Light for the Journey

Morning and Evening Prayers for Living Into God's World

by Christine Sine

Mustard Seed Associates

To the Mustard Seed House and
all those seeking connection to the
rhythms of God's world.

Table of Contents

Introduction

"It took Jesus a thousand years to die," proclaim Rita Nakashima Brock and Rebecca Ann Parker in their fascinating book *Saving Paradise: How Christianity Traded Love of This World for Crucifixion and Empire*. Brock and Parker traveled the Mediterranean looking for early Christian art that depicted the crucifixion, instead they found wonderful images of healing, restoration, and resurrection in a garden of incredible beauty. If the cross was portrayed, it was always in the background with Jesus in front of it, welcoming the repentant and reconciled into God's transformed resurrection world. The importance of the cross lay in the fact that it introduced people into God's new world of abundance and wholeness. For early Christians baptism was seen as an entry into paradise: "Through this ritual Christians gained entrance into the garden of God, which stood beyond the open doors of every church."[1]

The authors contend that images of Christ dying on the cross as the central focus of Christian faith grew out of the sanctioning of war and violence as a holy pursuit. The earliest images focusing on Christ's death that they found appeared in the tenth century in northern Europe and proliferated throughout the Middle Ages. What brought about this change? Brock and Parker believe that it was Charlemagne who began the trend as he spread Christianity by war and violence, subduing the Saxons and forcing them to become Christians. When Pope Urban sanctioned the first Crusade it further elevated violence to a practice that leads to salvation and placed images of the suffering, dying Christ firmly at the center of Christian faith. Though the Protestant reformation focused more on the empty cross and the risen Christ it still lacked the anticipation of God's resurrection world so vividly expressed in early Christian art.

I believe that we need to regain our focus. God's grand plan is not for war and violence with an end-times cataclysm of death and destruction, but rather a renewal of the earth and all its creatures and the restoration of the abundance, mutual concern and love of God's original creation. The hope of the New Testament is this life-affirming promise of a new heaven and a new earth in which wholeness and abundance come for all creation.[2] Old Testament prophets looked forward to this hope. It is the promise the apostles proclaimed, igniting the early church with such fervor that believers radically reoriented their priorities. Today we too are invited to live into this resurrection-created world as we seek to follow a Christ who defeated death and transfigured the world with

---

1. Rita Nakashima Brock and Rebecca Ann Parker, *Saving Paradise: How Christianity Traded Love of This World for Crucifixion and Empire* (Beacon Press, 2008), 115.

2. Revelation 21:1-4

the Spirit of life. It is the resurrected Christ who invites us to join him in making life flourish in all dimensions of wholeness and shalom.

At the core of Mustard Seed Associates is our belief in God's dream for the redemption and restoration of all the dimensions of life that were distorted and corrupted by the Fall. Our intimacy with God will be restored, our mutually caring relationships to each other will be re-established, our inner being will be renewed and our responsibility for stewardship of God's creation will be reinstated. Through the redemptive work of Christ, one day together with sisters and brothers of every culture and from every age, we will be made whole and live together in the love, joy, and mutual concern of God's original creation.

In *Light for the Journey: Morning and Evening Prayers for Living Into God's World*, you are invited to journey together with sisters and brothers from around the world into a rhythm of morning and evening prayer. This rhythm is intended to help us connect our daily prayers to the values of God's resurrection world in a way that strengthens our foundational beliefs and equips us to become part of God's mustard seed conspiracy, making a kingdom difference in God's world.

The Great Disconnect

I began my own Christian journey at an Interschool Christian Fellowship camp as a fifteen-year-old high school student back in the mid-sixties. I still vividly remember sitting on a bluff overlooking the Lane Cove River just outside Sydney, my senses filled with the aroma of eucalyptus leaves, my head swimming with new ideas and the conviction of my sin. It was a transforming experience that totally revolutionized my life. Within days of my decision, my newfound companions gifted me with a copy of Scripture Union's daily devotional and scripture reading plan. These wonderful resources fed my hungry soul over the next few years as I avidly read through the Bible and gained a beginner's insight into the wonder of God's story. I thank God for this early grounding in daily prayer and Bible study that gave me such wonderful resources for my Christian walk.

However a few years ago I realized that often my spiritual life suffered from chronic randomness. Though I regularly read through the entire Bible, I lacked a cohesive plan to connect my spiritual observances to God's dream of wholeness. I had no clear vision of God's resurrection-created world or of God's purposes for my life.

In addition, I am ashamed to say, I often saw my morning quiet time as a stand-alone experience that was meant to give me brownie points with God. The moment I closed my Bible, I became a functional atheist going about my daily routines as though God was still shut up in the Bible I had left at my desk. It is only in recent years that I have viewed my morning observances more as preparation for encounters with God in the day ahead. Slowly I am becoming aware of God's presence in the faces of friends and strangers, in the natural world and even in the mundane acts of washing the dishes, driving the car, and walking the dog.

Many followers of Christ suffer from this same disconnect between their spiritual practices and their everyday life. This separation severely disrupts the daily spiritual rhythms needed for healthy living, and we don't even notice: "Normal is getting dressed in clothes that you buy for work, driving through traffic in a car you are still paying for, in order to get to the job that you need so you can pay for the clothes, car, and the house that you leave empty all day in order to afford to live in it."[3] Strawberries in winter, apples in summer, central air and heat, and electric lights all encourage us to ignore God's rhythms.

Increasingly, daily routines are not only disconnected from God's rhythms but compete with them as well. Our 24/7 world demands more time and resources, convincing us that we can never slow down or take a break. It replaces the holy rituals of our faith with quasi-religious observances that seduce us with their seeming significance. We dismiss the idea of fasting during Lent, but go on obsessive spring diets instead. We rarely celebrate the seasons of the church calendar, but are inspired instead by gala sales at the local mall or by our passion for World Cup soccer or World Series baseball. The life, death, and resurrection of Christ is totally irrelevant to our daily activities. Church and spiritual practices add to our busyness and are often dumped when we get exhausted.

Tragically this lack of spiritual rhythm comes at a high cost. Anxiety, depression, and suicide are skyrocketing, and growing evidence suggests stress and pressure of overbooked schedules are major contributors. Even physical illnesses like high blood pressure and the common cold are impacted by our spiritual well being.

---

3. John De Graaf, David Wann, and Thomas H Naylor, *Affluenza: The All-Consuming Epidemic* (San Francisco, Calif.: Berrett-Koehler Publishers, 2001), 36.

Surprisingly, spiritual hunger is increasing especially amongst young people. Many of them are looking back to the life of Jesus and ancient monastic traditions, creatively adapting these practices to the modern world. They may not go for celibate living and bald eagle, tonsured hairdos, but they do crave a 24/7 spiritual rhythm that impacts all we are and do.

We want our faith to shape not just our prayers but also our work, play, and even financial decisions. We crave good, healthy practices that focus us on God's purposes for our lives and our world.

Beyond Chronic Randomness

In order to move our devotional life beyond its chronic randomness, we need life rhythms that intentionally renew our hope in God's kingdom vision and connect us to the essential foundations of our faith. Only then can the Holy Spirit work to shape how we allocate time and use resources with God's priorities in mind.

In *Surprised by Hope: Rethinking Heaven, the Resurrection, and the Mission of the Church*, British theologian NT Wright asserts that Christianity's most distinctive idea is bodily resurrection. After his resurrection, Jesus was a flesh-and-blood person. Wright contends that we will be raised into flesh and blood too. He further argues that if we truly believe this, then it will impact the way we live our lives now. If God intends to renew all of creation and all of life—a process already begun in the resurrection of Jesus—then our responsibility as Christians is to anticipate this renewal by working for hope and healing in today's world:

> So how can we learn to live as wide-awake people, as Easter people? . . . In particular if Lent is a time to give things up, Easter ought to be a time to take things up. . . . If Calvary means putting to death things in your life that need killing off if you are to flourish as a Christian and as a truly human being, then Easter should mean planting, watering, and training up things in your life (personal and corporate) that ought to be blossoming, filling the garden with color and perfume and in due course bearing fruit."[4]

The good news of the gospel is that we don't need to wait to see God's wholeness come into being:

> Jesus is risen, therefore God's new world has begun. Jesus is risen, therefore Israel and the world have been redeemed. Jesus is risen, therefore his followers have a new job to do. And what is that new job? To bring the life of heaven to birth in actual, physical earthly reality."[5]

Unfortunately most of us live in a very different world, unaware of the hope this resurrection-created world offers us for today. The quiet rhythms of prayer and Bible study that should connect us to God and God's world are drowned out by the strident shouts of our fast-paced cyber world. A glut of brilliant images cascades out of our HD screens at ever increasing speed. Church competes with our favorite sports and shopping trips.

Many of us suspect there should be more to life in Christ but don't know how to change. We are swamped by new Bible versions to read, endless spiritual websites to explore, and

---

4. NT Wright, *Surprised by Hope: Rethinking Heaven, the Resurrection, and the Mission of the Church* (New York: HarperOne, 2008), 255-257.
   5. Ibid., 293.

countless Christian artists to enjoy, yet we pray less, read the Bible less, and spend less time at church or involved in Christian service.

How do we find God's purposes for our lives and balance the urgent demands of our busy world with our commitment to Christ? We all struggle with these questions, but many sincere Christians have lost sight of God's vision and lack the spiritual rhythms and practices needed to maintain a Godly focus for their lives.

Daily rhythms are essential to life. Plants and ani-mals all respond to the cycle of light and dark. Biological rhythms pulse through our bodies in time to the same beat. When we wake, hormones spring into action, stimulating our hearts, raising our temperature, and adjusting our breathing. They nudge us to eat or exercise, encouraging us to develop physical routines in synch with their unconscious prompt-ings. Other hormones prompt us to relax and sleep. These rhythms repeat daily, adjusting to the yearly seasons and changing length of day.

Daily rhythms are rooted deep within the creation story. On the first day of creation God formed a rhythm of light and darkness: "God called the light 'day' and the darkness he called 'night.' And there was evening, and there was morn-ing—the first day" (Genesis 1:5, TNIV). This rhythm formed the basis for God's continuing acts of creation and still gov-erns most activity within the natural world. It also formed the foundation for the Jew-ish rhythm of prayer: "As for me, I call to God, and the Lord saves me. Evening, morning and noon I cry out in my distress and he hears my voice" (Psalm 55:16, TNIV).

The early church adopted this rhythm, gathering daily for prayer and fellowship. According to Gerald Sittser in his compelling book *Water From a Deep Well*, "Though this rhythm borrowed heavily from Judaism, it was clearly adapted to the new reality of Jesus Christ. The history and practices of Judaism receded into the background; the incarnation, death, and resurrection of Jesus became the centerpiece."[6] The monastic movements that followed also used a daily rhythm of prayer and work that they believed nurtured spiritual growth and facilitated the restoration of the image of God in sinful humans.[7]

The daily cycle of light and dark is not the only rhythm uncovered in the creation story that has relevance for our weekly cycle. The high point of the week for Jews and early Christians was the Sabbath, which provided purpose and focus for the rest of the week.

Tragically, today Sabbath is often little more than a set of legalistic rules. I once visited a small Scottish village in which the children's swings were still tied down on Saturday evening to prevent children playing on Sunday. For others, Sunday is the only day with the freedom to do almost anything we want. Our lives are too busy and our appetites too insatiable to consider losing a whole day that could be dedicated to work, play, or shopping.

For Jewish philosopher Abraham Heschel, the essence of the world to come is Sabbath eternal; the seventh day is a fore-

---

6. Gerald Sittser, *Water From a Deep Well: Christian Spirituality from Early Martyrs to Modern Missionaries*, (Downers Grove, Intervarsity Press, 2007), 100.

7. Ibid., 103.

taste of eternity.[8] When we practice Sabbath as God intended, we glimpse the joy, tranquility, peace, and abundance of God's eternal world. How sad that most of us do not embrace this privilege and incorporate it into the rhythm of our lives!

No wonder Jesus performed so many miracles on the Sabbath and criticized the legalistic Pharisaical rules that robbed people of their joy and freedom. He wasn't downplaying its importance but was giving breathtaking glimpses of that hoped-for eternal shalom world where all will be healed, fed, and provided for. Imagine how different our lives would be if we viewed the Sabbath this way—not just a day of rest but one of rejoicing in God, enjoying our restored relationships with others, and feasting on the glories of God's creation.

Living Into the Shalom of Sabbath

The Jews yearned for a future in which Sabbath was a way of life seven days a week. Early Christians believed that through Christ's resurrection, the wholeness of this eternal *shalom* world had arrived. Living together in loving communities that embraced widows and orphans, fed the poor, nursed the sick, and shared resources drew them into God's resurrection-created world. Sabbath celebrated both their renewed relationship to God and the glimpses they had caught of God's eternal world. They rested in the satisfaction of deeds that had brought God's wholeness and abundance and looked forward to how they could represent God's shalom world in the coming week.

---

8. Abraham Heschel, *The Sabbath* (New York: Farrar, Straus and Giroux, 1951), 74.

Shalom living doesn't come easily. It requires a redirection of our entire lives, not just on Sunday but every day. The purpose of this book is to facilitate this reorientation by providing a rhythm of daily prayer that moves beyond chronic randomness and enables us to connect intentionally to God and to the foundations of God's resurrection-created world 24/7.

In *Light for the Journey: Morning and Evening Prayers for Living into God's World*, I have taken what I see as the seven essential foundations of resurrection, shalom faith and used each as a theme for one day of the week. I am indebted to David Adam's book *The Rhythm of Life*, which first introduced me to this idea and exposed me to liturgical prayers like this. Rather than using a different theme for each day of the week, you might also like to focus on one theme for an entire week and then move on to the next.

The secular consumer culture constantly reminds us of its values and tries to draw us into its practices. We need equally powerful ways to connect us to God's values that draw us into the practices of God's world.

Sunday's theme begins the week with the celebration of Sabbath and anticipation of God's eternal shalom world. We rejoice in this vision of wholeness and abundance which will one day be completely fulfilled in Christ.

On **Monday** we focus on our restored relationship to God our Creator and the call to be stewards of God's creation. The gospel always comes to us in the midst of the created world, which was made through Jesus Christ and is being recreated through him.

On **Tuesday** our focus shifts to Christ our Savior and what it means to carry his incarnational presence into our world. As Christ's followers, we are called to live out the claims of the gospel.

Wednesday focuses on the in-dwelling Holy Spirit who equips us with the gifts and abilities to carry out the gospel call as God's servants and proclaimers of God's resurrection-created world.

On **Thursday** our reflections turn towards community and what it means to be part of God's eternal family from every tribe and nation, rich and poor, male and female.

Friday reflects on the Cross and the wholeness achieved through repentance, forgiveness, and reconciliation.

We conclude the week on **Saturday** with a focus on the kingdom of God and the clouds of witnesses who have gone before us.

Each theme provides a short reflection followed by a brief focusing exercise with questions and suggested prayer topics. This is intended to encourage you to incorporate the theme into your activities throughout the day. I suggest that you rotate through each of the focusing points over a period of weeks. This is a great way to calm your thoughts and quiet your mind. You might also like to rotate through the prayer points and make a list of specific people, organizations, or geographic areas to pray for.

Each section ends with morning and evening prayers intended to draw you into God's presence, strengthen the foundations of your faith and send you out to do God's work in the world. Scriptures are usually quoted in contemporary versions like the Message or the New Living Translation. I find these connect more easily to the world we live in and enable children to participate with their parents in reciting the prayers. Ricci and Eliacín Rosario-Kilmer's seven-year-old daughter Catie loves to participate in morning prayers at the Mustard Seed House. She already knows many of the responses by heart and is slowly committing the scriptures to memory as well. Even three-year-old Gabriel is beginning to join in some of the responses. What a great way for kids to learn the foundations of their faith!

After some of the scripture readings there are community responses that are drawn from the readings. You may, however, rather use the more traditional responses like when the reader says, "The word of the Lord," everyone responds, "**Thanks be to God**." The traditional responses associated with gospel readings are "The gospel of the Lord," "**Praise to you, Lord Jesus Christ**."

I keep a loose-leaf folder divided into the same daily themes of this book beside me when I pray. If I read or hear something that adds to my insights on a theme, I write it down. Over the years I have gathered a rich assortment of Bible verses, spiritual quotes, and excerpts from sermons and books that have greatly enriched my faith and moved me to a deeper understanding of God and God's purposes. Reading through my reflections is particularly helpful when I am going through times of struggle or need encouragement.

Our faith should not be a passive expression of our love for God, but rather an active participation in God's work to change our world. These prayers are meant for use in a small group or community but can easily be used alone. They are not meant to be rushed through, however. The prayers are designed to renew the foundations of our faith on a weekly basis, and so it is important to still our minds and enter into a quiet place in which it is easy to imagine God is in our midst.

"Prayer restores us to God: work allows us to participate in God's restoration of the world."[9] Unless we learn to live into this healthy rhythm and apply ourselves with this kind of intentionality, we will never mature into the people that God intends us to be.

---

9. Sittser, *Water From a Deep Well*, 114.

Sunday

Living Into a Resurrection-Created World

When Rory Dunn's Humvee was blown up by explosives in Iraq during deployment, Rory suffered an open-head injury that left him brain-damaged, deaf, and almost blind. Only his mother Cynthia believed he would ever regain consciousness or be capable of a normal life. She sat beside his comatose body pleading with him not to die, and when he opened his eyes six weeks later, Cynthia worked to restore his independence. She played games with him to exercise his brain. She corrected him when he made inappropriate remarks and pushed him to wash his clothes and handle his money. Due largely to Cynthia's belief that a better life was possible for her son, Rory's recovery has far exceeded doctors' expectations, and he is now able to live on his own.[10]

Do we believe a better world is possible? Can we imagine God's resurrection-created world in which the blind see, the deaf hear, and the hungry are fed? If not, then we will never learn to live into that world or see it come into reality. Sunday, the first day of the week, celebrates our anticipation of God's new world. It anchors our lives in God's dream for a world in which wholeness, peace, and abundance are restored for all creation. It focuses on all we are and do and gives meaning and purpose to the rest of the week as we picture how to use our time and resources to bring glimpses of God's new world into being.

The Sabbath day is a time for gratitude and rejoicing. Just as God rested on the seventh day to enjoy the fruits of six days of hard labor and exalt in the satisfaction of a job well done, so should we. We rest in God's approval and pleasure at what we have accomplished that bears the fingerprints of our awe-inspiring God.

First we rejoice in our restored fellowship with God. Sunday is time to enjoy God and bask in God's love and approval. My husband Tom and I relax over breakfast and update our journals. I particularly like to reflect on where I have sensed God's approval and how well I have maintained God's priorities. This practice draws on the Prayer of Examen, which encourages us to reflect on each day and examine where the Holy Spirit has both instructed and corrected us.[11] I also look ahead and consider ways to draw closer to God and better express God's love in the future. This process has greatly increased my sensitivity to the leading of God's Spirit in my life. It has also made me more aware of the areas in which my own spirit is still in conflict with God's guidance.

---

10. Barry Yeoman, "When Wounded Vets Come Home," *AARP Magazine* (July & August 2008) 46-53.

11. For a good description of the Prayer of Examen, see http://norprov.org/spirituality/ignatianprayer.htm

Restored fellowship with God cannot be confined to individual refreshment, however. We stand before God as a worshipping community of believers from every tribe and nation and culture. Celebrating our restored fellowship with God must also incorporate coming together with a worshipping community of fellow believers. This is the second celebration of Sunday. It is a time to enjoy restored relationships with friends, family, and our neighbors near and far—that great international community that is Christ's body.

We are all included in God's eternal shalom community. As we go to church or interact with people from other cultures and backgrounds, we savor the rich diversity of God's family and the joy of sharing life with brothers and sisters from every tribe and culture. In sharing the bread and wine of communion, we are united not just with believers around the world, but also with all those who have gone before us. At the same time we may be confronted with the pain of those for whom Sabbath is still little more than a dream—the destitute, the abandoned, and the neglected.

Thirdly, the Sabbath is a day to celebrate God's glorious created world. This is a great day to go for a hike, drive in the country, or get out into the garden and savor its breathtaking beauty and rich fragrance. I love to imagine that our Creator walks in my garden with me, enjoying the beauty of all I see.

Focusing Our Thoughts

Set aside time during the day to reflect on the past week and prepare for the week ahead. Express your gratitude to God for good things accomplished in and through you that bear God's fingerprints. Here are some ideas that may help you to focus:

- Begin with silence reflecting on the meaning of God's eternal Sabbath world. Create a picture in your mind of what you think God's resurrection-created world will look like.

   1. Where have you experienced Christ's resurrection power over the last week?

   2. Where have you felt closest to God and to God's eternal world?

   3. Where has God's resurrection power flowed through you to touch others and bring them new life?

   4. How have you enabled others to enter the peace, abundance, and freedom of God's resurrection-created world?

   5. What aspects of God's eternal world do you want to model through your life and faith community in the coming week?

   6. How in this coming week can you draw closer to God and better express God's love and compassion?

- Picture times throughout the day when you plan to stop and thank God for the eternal shalom world of wholeness, abundance, and mutual care we now catch glimpses of that will one day fully come into being.

Focusing Our Prayers

- Express prayers of gratitude and thanksgiving for:

   1. Where you have caught glimpses of God and of God's eternal shalom world this last week.

   2. Restored closeness to God and your awareness of God's presence in and around you.

   3. Renewed family bonds and friendships that assure you of God's presence with you and your loved ones.

   4. Insights from other cultures that have given you glimpses of God's shalom world.

   5. The glory of God's created world and the glimpses it has given you of God.

   6. Places in which you have seen God's eternal world break into the lives of the oppressed, sick, hungry and marginalized.

   7. Those who have drawn closer to the saving and redemptive power of Christ this week.

Morning Prayer

Jesus, we awake to the joy of life,
You are in our midst and call us by name,
You are risen from the dead. Alleluia!
The night is gone the day is come,
We live in your resurrection light,
You are risen from the dead. Alleluia!
We put off the deeds of darkness,
And take on the ways of life,
You are risen from the dead. Alleluia!
May we clothe ourselves with Christ,
And awake to the joy of God's life within us,
You are risen from the dead. Alleluia!

> *Pause to reflect on the abundance, joy, and peace of God's resurrection-created world.*

Christ, awaken us to the joy of your life within us,
Open our eyes that we might welcome your presence,
Open our lips that we might declare your praise,
Open our hearts that we might share your compassion,
Christ, awaken us to the joy of your life within us.

Te Deum Laudamus[12]

You are God, and we praise you,
You are the Lord, and we acclaim you,
You are the eternal Father,
All creation worships you.
To you all angels, all the powers of heaven,
Cherubim and seraphim sing in endless praise.
Holy, holy, holy Lord, God of power and might,

---

12. "Te Deum,"is a traditional hymn of joy and thanksgiving accredited to Nicetas, Bishop of Remesiana (4th century).

Heaven and earth are full of your glory.
The glorious company of apostles praises you,
The noble fellowship of prophets praise you,
The white-robed army of martyrs praises you.
Throughout the world the holy Church acclaims you.
Father of majesty unbounded,
Your true and only Son, worthy of all worship,
And the Holy Spirit, advocate and guide.
You Christ are the King of glory,
The eternal Son of the Father.
When you became man to set us free,
You did not abhor the Virgin's womb.
You overcame the sting of death,
And opened the kingdom of heaven to all believers.
You are seated at God's right hand in glory,
We believe that you will come and be our judge.
Come then Lord and help your people,
Bought with the price of your own blood,
And bring us with your saints to glory everlasting.

Adapted from Philippians 2:5-11 (Message)

Jesus Christ was truly God, but did not try to remain equal with God,
Instead he gave up everything and became a slave.
All creation on earth and in heaven will call out in praise to Jesus Christ.
He lived a selfless, obedient life and then died a selfless, obedient death,
He died the worst kind of death the death of crucifixion.
All creation on earth and in heaven will call out in praise to Jesus Christ.
Because of his obedience God has lifted him high,
And honored him far above all other creatures.
All creation on earth and in heaven will call out in praise to Jesus Christ.

So that at the name of Jesus every knee shall bow in worship,
And all creation in heaven and on earth will call out in praise to his name.

All creation on earth and in heaven will call out in praise to Jesus Christ,

Glory and honor to God the Father almighty, to the Son and the Holy Spirit,

As it was in the beginning is now and shall be forever, Amen.

All creation on earth and in heaven will call out in praise to Jesus Christ.

Romans 5:1-11 (Message)

By entering through faith into what God has always wanted to do for us—set us right with him, make us fit for him—we have it all together with God because of our Master Jesus. And that's not all: We throw open our doors to God and discover at the same moment that he has already thrown open his door to us. We find ourselves standing where we always hoped we might stand—out in the wide open spaces of God's grace and glory, standing tall and shouting our praise.

There's more to come: We continue to shout our praise even when we're hemmed in with troubles, because we know how troubles can develop passionate patience in us, and how that patience in turn forges the tempered steel of virtue, keeping us alert for whatever God will do next. In alert expectancy such as this, we're never left feeling shortchanged. Quite the contrary—we can't round up enough containers to hold everything God generously pours into our lives through the Holy Spirit!

Christ arrives right on time to make this happen. He didn't, and doesn't, wait for us to get ready. He presented himself for this sacrificial death when we were far too weak and rebellious to do anything to get ourselves ready. And even if we hadn't been so weak, we wouldn't have known what to do anyway. We can understand someone dying for a person worth dying for, and we can understand how someone good and noble could inspire us to selfless sacrifice. But God put his love on the line for us by offering his Son in sacrificial death while we were of no use whatever to him.

Now that we are set right with God by means of this sacrificial death, the consummate blood sacrifice, there is no longer a question of being at odds with God in any way. If, when we were at our worst, we were put on friendly terms with God by the sacrificial death of his Son, now that we're at our best, just think of how our lives will expand and deepen by means of his resurrection life! Now that we have actually received this amazing friendship with God, we are no longer content to simply say it in plodding prose. We sing and shout our praises to God through Jesus, the Messiah!

Come, let's sing and shout our praises to God through Jesus, the Messiah!

John 20:19-31(Message)

Later on that day, the disciples had gathered together, but, fearful of the Jews, had locked all the doors in the house. Jesus entered, stood among them, and said, "Peace to you." Then he showed them his hands and side. The disciples, seeing the Master with their own eyes, were exuberant. Jesus repeated his greeting: "Peace to you. Just as the Father sent me, I send you." Then he took a deep breath and breathed into them. "Receive the Holy Spirit," he said. "If you forgive someone's sins, they're gone for good. If you don't forgive sins, what are you going to do with them?"

But Thomas, sometimes called the Twin, one of the Twelve, was not with them when Jesus came. The other disciples told him, "We saw the Master." But he said, "Unless I see the nail holes in his hands, put my finger in the nail holes, and stick my hand in his side, I won't believe it." Eight days later, his disciples were again in the room. This time Thomas was with them. Jesus came through the locked doors, stood among them, and said, "Peace to you." Then he focused his attention on Thomas. "Take your finger and examine my hands. Take your hand and stick it in my side. Don't be unbelieving. Believe." Thomas said, "My Master! My God!" Jesus said, "So, you believe because you've seen with your own eyes. Even better blessings are in store for those who believe without seeing."

Jesus provided far more God-revealing signs than are written down in this book. These are written down so you will believe that Jesus is the Messiah, the Son of God, and in the act of believing, have real and eternal life in the way he personally revealed it.

Jesus Christ, we believe you are the Messiah, Son of the living God,
You are the one who raises the dead to life,
You are the Prince of Peace, the Savior of our world,
The one in whom all creation finds its true purpose.
Jesus Christ, we believe that you have come to bring us new life,
Everyone who has faith in you will live even if they die,
We stand in the wide open spaces of God's grace and glory.
Alleluia, we sing and shout our praises to Jesus Christ our Messiah
You are risen from the dead and have given us new life.

God who brings us life and freedom,
Have mercy on us.
Christ who shows us love and peace,
Have mercy on us.
Spirit who fills us with comfort and compassion,
Grant us peace.

Our Father in heaven, hallowed be your name. Your Kingdom come, your will be done, on earth as in heaven. Give us today our daily bread. Forgive us our sins, as we forgive those who sin against us. Lead us not into temptation, but deliver us from evil. For the kingdom, the power and the glory are yours. Now and forever. Amen

Pause to offer specific prayers and thanksgivings.

Lord Jesus Christ, we shout for joy at the resurrection,
And rejoice because you have triumphed over the grave.
Risen Christ, you give us hope.
We stand with those in doubt and despair,
Believing they will be transformed by your light.
Risen Christ, you give us hope.
We embrace those who are troubled in mind,
Believing they will be enfolded in your peace.

Risen Christ, you give us hope.
We grieve with those in pain and distress,
Believing they will be healed by your loving touch.
Risen Christ, you give us hope.
We encourage those who care for the sick,
Believing they will be anointed with your healing power.
Risen Christ, you give us hope.
We weep with those who mourn,
Believing they will discover the joy of eternal life.
Risen Christ, you give us hope.

Risen Christ, we live today in anticipation of your resurrection-
    created world,
We live in the hope of your forgiveness,
We live in expectation of your healing,
We live in the assurance of your salvation,
Risen Christ, we will live in anticipation of your resurrection-
    created world.
Risen Christ, we take on your life today,
A life of loving and caring,
A life of healing and wholeness,
A life of sharing and giving,
Risen Christ, we take on your life today.

We will go into the week with compassion and love,
Knowing we are touched by the God of life,
May our lives shine with the holiness of God,
May our hearts be transformed by the glory of Christ,
May our ways be filled with the joy of the Spirit.
The love of almighty God surround you,
The peace of the risen Christ indwell you,
The fellowship of the Spirit unite you,
The life of the Triune God be yours,
This day and evermore,
Amen.

Evening Prayer

God of peace and love,
God of joy and celebration,
We gather to sing your praises.
We rejoice with the angels,
We stand united with the saints,
We shout aloud Alleluia!

> *Silence for lighting the candle. Reflect on where you have connected to God and God's resurrection-created world today.*

To God above us, creator and sustainer of all life,
To Christ all around us, Redeemer and Savior of our world,
To Spirit deep within us, Seal of our inheritance, promise of
    abundant life,
Praise and glory to you forever.

We sing for joy tonight and rest secure in God's promise,
The ruler of all worlds, the shepherd of creation,
Jesus Christ has risen from the dead and given us new life.
He comes not in power, not in might,
But in the gentleness of love.
He is not far off where none can touch him,
But is everywhere present in our world,
He is in the face of all to whom we speak,
In the voice of all who speak to us.
He walks beside us as a friend, before us as a guide,
Behind us as a shield.
Praise God! Jesus Christ is risen from the dead!
And has given us new life.

Psalm 96 (NLT)

Sing a new song to the Lord! Let the whole earth sing to the Lord! Sing to the Lord; praise his name. Each day proclaim the good news that he saves. Publish his glorious deeds among the nations. Tell everyone about the amazing things he does. Great is the Lord! He is most worthy of praise! He is to be feared above all gods. The gods of other nations are mere idols, but the Lord made the heavens! Honor and majesty surround him; strength and beauty fill his sanctuary.

O nations of the world, recognize the Lord; recognize that the Lord is glorious and strong. Give to the Lord the glory he deserves! Bring your offering and come into his courts. Worship the Lord in all his holy splendor. Let all the earth tremble before him. Tell all the nations, "The Lord reigns!" The world stands firm and cannot be shaken. He will judge all peoples fairly.

Let the heavens be glad, and the earth rejoice! Let the sea and everything in it shout his praise! Let the fields and their crops burst out with joy! Let the trees of the forest rustle with praise before the Lord, for he is coming! He is coming to judge the earth. He will judge the world with justice, and the nations with his truth.

Let the whole world sing a new song to the Lord

Adapted from Isaiah 9:2-7 (NLT)

The people who walk in darkness will see a great light. For those who live in a land of deep darkness, a light will shine.

You will enlarge the nation of Israel, and its people will rejoice. They will rejoice before you as people rejoice at the harvest and like warriors dividing the plunder.

For you will break the yoke of their slaveryand lift the heavy burden from their shoulders. You will break the oppressor's rod, just as you did when you destroyed the army of Midian.

The boots of the warrior and the uniforms bloodstained by war will all be burned. They will be fuel for the fire.

For a child is born to us, a son is given to us. The government will rest on his shoulders. And he will be called: Wonderful Counselor, Mighty God, Everlasting Father, Prince of Peace. His government and its peace will never end. He will rule with fairness and justice from the throne of his ancestor David for all eternity.

The passionate commitment of the Lord of Heaven's Armies will make this happen!

Hallelujah, Jesus Christ will rule with fairness and justice.

2 Corinthians 5:14-21 (Message)

Our firm decision is to work from this focused center: One man died for everyone. That puts everyone in the same boat. He included everyone in his death so that everyone could also be included in his life, a resurrection life, a far better life than people ever lived on their own.

Because of this decision we don't evaluate people by what they have or how they look. We looked at the Messiah that way once and got it all wrong, as you know. We certainly don't look at him that way anymore. Now we look inside, and what we see is that anyone united with the Messiah gets a fresh start, is created new. The old life is gone; a new life burgeons! Look at it! All this comes from the God who settled the relationship between us and him, and then called us to settle our relationships with each other. God put the world square with himself through the Messiah, giving the world a fresh start by offering forgiveness of sins. God has given us the task of telling everyone what he is doing. We're Christ's representatives. God uses us to persuade men and women to drop their differences and enter into God's work of making things right between them. We're speaking for Christ himself now: Become friends with God; he's already a friend with you. How? You ask. In Christ. God put the wrong on him who never did anything wrong, so we could be put right with God.

Praise God, in Christ the old life is gone, and a new life has come into being.

John 11:21-27 (Message)

Martha said, "Master, if you'd been here, my brother wouldn't have died. Even now, I know that whatever you ask God he will give you." Jesus said, "Your brother will be raised up." Martha replied, "I know that he will be raised up in the resurrection at the end of time." "You don't have to wait for the End. I am, right now, Resurrection and Life. The one who believes in me, even though he or she dies, will live. And everyone who lives believing in me does not ultimately die at all. Do you believe this?"

"Yes, Master. All along I have believed that you are the Messiah, the Son of God who comes into the world."

Jesus, we believe that you are the Messiah who has given us new life.

We have lived this day in anticipation of your resurrection-created world,
Where your eternal Sabbath rest waits for all creation.
We remember your promise of renewal and rebirth for all life.
Your Sabbath rest is all-inclusive.
You promise to take our yoke upon you,
Your Sabbath rest shares our burdens.
You promise to set the captives free,
Your Sabbath rest frees from oppression.
You promise to feed the hungry,
Your Sabbath rest brings abundance for all.
You promise to heal the sick,
Your Sabbath rest brings us wholeness.
Not alone, but together,
A great international community that is your body,
We live in expectation of that day when Christ returns,
And your eternal Sabbath rest comes for all creation.

Our Father in heaven, hallowed be your name. Your Kingdom come, your will be done, on earth as in heaven. Give us today our daily bread. Forgive us our sins, as we forgive those who sin against us. Lead us not into temptation, but deliver us from evil. For the kingdom, the power and the glory are yours. Now and forever. Amen

Pause to offer specific prayers and thanksgivings.

God who offers rest to the weary,
May we breathe deeply of your serenity.
God who promises to shoulder our burdens,
May we release our heavy loads to you.

God who comes in the midst of tired moments,
Come down, refresh and renew our souls.
Allow us to touch the quiet essence of you,
Within us, around us, behind us, before us.
May we trust in your abundant love,
May we rest in the assurance of your salvation.

God, as the night descends,
You grant us the gift of sleep.
We rest knowing your light has come into the world,
And the darkness will not odvercome it.
We are graced by the wonder of Christ's presence,
We are filled with the tenderness of his love.
We rest in the anticipation of your new world,
Where love, joy, peace, and abundance abound.
Calm us, Lord, as you calmed the storm,
Still us, Lord, and keep us from harm.
We rest in the calm of your presence,
Enfold us in your peace and grant us rest.
Amen.

Monday

God, Creation, and the Call to Stewardship

In the last few years I have become a passionate gardener spurred on by our small community at the Mustard Seed House where we endeavour to grow as many of our own vegetables as we can on a small urban lot. To me there is nothing more satisfying than walking out in the early morning to pick a crisp head of lettuce or a handful of sweet tomatoes for a luncheon salad. And there is nothing quite like a peach eaten fresh from the tree.

We begin the work week celebrating God the Creator who formed not only us, but all creation. It is encouraging to remember that God loves our world, lives in it and is revealed through every aspect of it. It is also important to remind ourselves that God's first job for humankind was to steward creation and make it prosper. Most of our world's population now lives in cities where so much of life is totally divorced from the natural world that we must make a deliberate effort to connect ourselves to the God revealed through creation. As God's people we are responsible to love the world with the same love that God has expressed through creation and as a consequence must accept God's call to be godly stewards of all that has already been created. "The LORD God took the man and put him in the Garden of Eden to work it and take care of it" (Genesis 2:15, TNIV).

Walking in the garden and being so intimately involved in God's creation has given me new insights into God's character. In nature I catch wonderful glimpses of God's overflowing love—a love so great that it created an infinite variety of living expressions in the plants, animals, and insects of our world. It is a love so all encompassing that it created unimagined complexity in the minutest detail of the atoms and cells that are the building blocks of life. It is a love so incomprehensible that it did not create robots, but formed creatures that could also love, care, suffer, and experience joy. It is a love so wonderful that it wanted to share the joy of life with its creation.

Creation proclaims God's faithfulness. We often take the breathtaking beauty of dawn, which heralds God's new day of promise, for granted. We rarely remember that God ordained the seasons, but we expect that summer will follow spring and autumn will give way to winter in its allotted place, enabling us to plant, to grow, and to harvest the abundance of God's provision. In faithfulness God pours out love in the complexity, beauty, and wonder of creation, assuring us that the God who made our earth will never abandon us.

Creation mirrors the overwhelming generosity of God. When we diligently work the earth—sow the seed in its season, fertilize, water. and nurture the plant into growth—we often reap a harvest so abundant that it is awe-inspiring.

God's harvest provides enough for our own needs and an abundance to give away and share. It is as miraculous as the feeding of the five thousand with the loaves and fish. It is as generous and rich as the most magnificent banquet ever set before a king. It is as satisfying as any accomplishment of our own efforts.

The overflowing abundance of God's harvest reminds us that it is God who accomplishes the work. We plant the seed and water the soil, but it is God who gives life—germinating seeds, growing plants, enriching the lush fruit and grain for harvest. Even through the dark cold days of winter, God is still at work, anchoring and strengthening roots, anticipating the day when all will burst out into luxuriant growth. Autumn-planted shrubs send down deeper and stronger roots than those planted in spring. God gives life to all our efforts, sustaining us through the seasons of toil and hard work until we reap God's abundant and generous harvest. Amazingly, we often claim God's harvest as our own, ignoring the One who provided it.

To be a good steward of creation has implications for every part of life. How can we express concern for creation and drive a gas guzzling vehicle that pollutes and destroys the environment? How can we waste the earth's resources by buying and consuming without concern for our ecological footprint? How can we love God and not preserve parks or not work for regional sustainability and the preservation of community and family farms? How can we not care about deforestation, the annihilation of rainforests, the devastation to nature caused by urban sprawl, or the loss of ecological diversity?

Focusing Our Thoughts

Set aside a few minutes during the day to enjoy nature and meditate on the revelation of God unveiled through the created world. Sit in a park at lunch time, pet your dog, admire the sunset, walk in your garden in the evening, or visit the local zoo or aquarium.

- What makes you aware of God's presence and God's voice:

    1. in the beauty of creation?

    2. in the rich diversity and unimaginable variety of the created world?

    3. in the rhythms that pulse through time and space, ordering the days and cycles of all created life?

- What do the seasons of the year teach you about the character of God?

- How is God revealed through the changing patterns and rhythm of the day?

    4. in the intricacy revealed in a human cell, an atom, a snowflake, and even a mathematical formula?

    5. in the interconnectedness of ecosystems and the interdependence of all creation?

- Picture times throughout the day when you plan to pause and praise God for the created world.

Focusing Our Prayers

- Pray for the church's ministry in stewardship of creation and for organizations involved in creation care.

- Pray for areas that suffer from natural disasters—for relief from famine, flood and fire.

- Pray for areas impacted by pollution, acid rain, global warming, and environmental degradation.

- Pray for farmers, fishermen, and horticulturalists, for the fruitfulness and abundance of their harvest.

- Pray for environmentalists, landscape gardeners, conservationists, and all who seek to preserve God's creation.

- Pray for creative vocations—artists, musicians, graphic designers, those in the fashion industry.

- Pray for God's creativity to be expressed in and through your life.

Morning Prayer

God of wind and storm, God of trees and flowers,
God of birds and beasts, God of men and women,
God who gave birth to all creation,
Come down this day and dwell among us.

Pause to reflect on God's glory in the created world.

God, your world is translucent,
Through all creation your glory shines.
God, all of life reflects your creative presence and sustaining love.
God, we see you in the wind and calm,
We see you in the sun and moon.
God, all of life reflects your creative presence and sustaining love.
God, we hear you in the song of birds and bees,
We hear you in the crash of waves and waterfalls,
God, all of life reflects your creative presence and sustaining love.
God, we feel you in warmth of sun and cold of ice,
We feel you in the richness of soil and softness of fur.
God, all of life reflects your creative presence and sustaining love.
God, we smell you in the perfume of rose and jasmine,
We smell you in the aroma of fresh cut apple and peach.
God, all of life reflects your creative presence and sustaining love.
God, we see you in the rich abundance of the harvest,
We hear you in the voices of those who enjoy its bounty.
God, all of life reflects your creative presence and sustaining love.
God, we feel you in the care of those with whom we share its generosity,
God, we know you in your love and care for all creation.

God, all of life reflects your creative presence and sustaining love.

Adapted from Psalm 65:5-12 (TNIV)

God, you call forth songs of joy from all the earth.
You answer us with awesome deeds of righteousness,
God our Savior, you are the hope of the ends of the earth.
You are the hope of the farthest seas,
When morning dawns and evening fades,
You call forth songs of joy.
God, you call forth songs of joy from all the earth.
You care for the land and water it,
You enrich it abundantly,
The streams of God are filled with water,
To provide the people with grain,
For so you have ordained it.
God, you call forth songs of joy from all the earth.
The whole earth is filled with awe at your wonder,
You drench its furrows and level its ridges,
You soften it with showers and bless its crops,
You crown the year with your bounty,
And your carts overflow with abundance.
God, you call forth songs of joy from all the earth.
The grasslands of the deserts overflow,
The hills are clothed with gladness,
The meadows are covered with flocks,
And the valleys are mantled with grain,
They shout for joy and sing.
God, you call forth songs of joy from all the earth.

Ezekiel 34:25-27 (CEV)

The LORD God said: The people of Israel are my sheep, and I solemnly promise that they will live in peace. I will chase away every wild animal from the desert and the forest, so my sheep will not be afraid. They will live around my holy mountain, and I will bless them by sending more than enough rain to make their trees produce fruit and their crops to grow. I will set them free from slavery and let them live safely in their own land. Then they will know that I am the LORD.

God will provide abundant food for all the people of the earth.

Colossians 1:15-20 (Message)

We look at this Son and see the God who cannot be seen. We look at this Son and see God's original purpose in everything created. For everything, absolutely everything, above and below, visible and invisible, rank after rank after rank of angels—everything got started in him and finds its purpose in him. He was there before any of it came into existence and holds it all together right up to this moment. And when it comes to the church, he organizes and holds it together, like a head does a body.

He was supreme in the beginning and—leading the resurrection parade—he is supreme in the end. From beginning to end he's there, towering far above everything, everyone. So spacious is he, so roomy, that everything of God finds its proper place in him without crowding. Not only that, but all the broken and dislocated pieces of the universe—people and things, animals and atoms—get properly fixed and fit together in vibrant harmonies, all because of his death, his blood that poured down from the cross.

In Christ all the broken and dislocated pieces of the universe are properly fixed.

Matthew 6:25-33 (Message)

If you decide for God, living a life of God-worship, it follows that you don't fuss about what's on the table at mealtimes or whether the clothes in your closet are in fashion. There is far more to your life than the food you put in your stomach, more to your outer appearance than the clothes you hang on your body. Look at the birds, free and unfettered, not tied down to a job description, careless in the care of God. And you count far more to him than birds.

Has anyone by fussing in front of the mirror ever gotten taller by so much as an inch? All this time and money wasted on fashion—do you think it makes that much difference? Instead of looking at the fashions, walk out into the fields and look at the wildflowers. They never primp or shop, but have you ever seen color and design quite like it? The ten best-dressed men and women in the country look shabby alongside them.

If God gives such attention to the appearance of wildflowers—most of which are never even seen—don't you think he'll attend to you, take pride in you, do his best for you? What I'm trying to do here is to get you to relax, to not be so preoccupied with getting, so you can respond to God's giving. People who don't know God and the way he works fuss over these things, but you know both God and how he works. Steep your life in God-reality, God-initiative, God-provisions. Don't worry about missing out. You'll find all your everyday human concerns will be met.

We believe in God above us,
Creator of all things, sustainer of all life.
We believe in Christ beside us,
Companion and friend, redeemer of all the broken pieces of
our universe.
We believe in Spirit deep within us,
Advocate and guide, who lives with us eternally.
We believe in God's resurrection created world,
Where all things are fixed, and all creation fits together in
vibrant harmonies.
We believe in God above, beside, within,
God yesterday, today and forever, the three in one, the one in
three,
We believe in God.

Our Father in heaven, hallowed be your name. Your King-
dom come, your will be done, on earth as in heaven. Give us
today our daily bread. Forgive us our sins, as we forgive those
who sin against us. Lead us not into temptation, but deliver
us from evil. For the kingdom, the power and the glory are
yours. Now and forever. Amen

Pause to offer specific prayers and thanksgivings.

Upon all farmers, market gardeners, foresters, and all who work the land,
Lord, have mercy.
Upon ranchers, zoo keepers, veterinarians, and all who work with animals,
Lord, have mercy.
Upon all fisherman, sailors, and all who work on the sea,
Lord, have mercy.
Upon all whose homes are destroyed by tsunami or earthquake or hurricane,
Christ, have mercy.
Upon all whose land has been spoiled by drought or flood or war,
Christ, have mercy.
Upon all those who suffer through pollution and destruction of creation,
Christ, have mercy.
Upon conservationists, park rangers, and all who care for God's good creation,
Lord, have mercy.
Upon landscape gardeners, horticulturalists, and all who preserve and restore the earth's beauty,
Lord, have mercy.
Upon all God's creatures, great and small, and on all who care for their environment,
Lord, have mercy.

God almighty, creator of all life, the One who fixes all the broken places of our universe, the work of your hands reflects your great love and concern for all creation. May we be wise stewards and ensure that nothing you have made is spoiled or misused. May we share generously and justly from your rich and abundant resources. Jesus Christ, who gave yourself for our world, unite us through your covenant of peace, so that all peoples of the earth may share your lavish bounty together.

Life of God be with you this day,
Love of the Creator fill your heart,
Light of the Savior guide your steps,
Hope of the Sanctifier teach your minds,
Life of the Three sustain you,
Love of the One encircle you,
Now and always, this day and forever,
Amen.

Evening Prayer

God who makes the crops to grow,
God who feeds the birds and beasts,
Refresh us this night and protect us from harm.
God who heals our wounds and pain,
God who brings us peace and rest,
Refresh us this night and protect us from harm.

> *Pause to reflect on what you have learned through God's
> created world today.*

For the music of our world,
The divine song that sings through all creation,
God our creator, we praise you.
For the beauty of all you have created,
A mirror of the wonders of heaven,
God our creator, we praise you.
For the resounding roar of thunder,
Your awesome majesty revealed,
God our creator, we praise you.
For a clouded sky splashed with sunset colors,
A glimpse of heaven's glory,
God our creator, we praise you.
For the fragrance of a rose,
Your sweet perfume of grace,
God our creator, we praise you.
For a riotous field of wildflowers,
God's exuberant laughter unfolded,
God our creator, we praise you.
For a snowflake, an atom, a mathematical formula,
A hint of your unimagined complexity,
God our creator, we praise you.
For the call to steward your creation,
To tend your garden and make it flourish,
God our creator, we praise you.

Psalm 148 (Message)

Alleluia! Praise God from heaven, praise him from the mountaintops;
Praise him, all you his angels, praise him, all you his warriors,
Praise him, sun and moon, praise him, you morning stars;
Praise him, high heaven, praise him, heavenly rain clouds;

Praise, oh let them praise the name of God—he spoke the word, and
there they were! He set them in place from all time to eternity; He gave
his orders, and that's it!

Praise God from earth, you sea dragons, you fathomless ocean deeps;
Fire and hail, snow and ice, hurricanes obeying his orders; Mountains
and all hills, apple orchards and cedar forests; Wild beasts and herds
of cattle, snakes, and birds in flight; Earth's kings and all races, leaders
and important people, Robust men and women in their prime, and yes,
graybeards and little children. Let them praise the name of God—it's the
only Name worth praising. His radiance exceeds anything in earth and
sky; he's built a monument—his very own people!

Praise from all who love God!   Israel's children, intimate friends of God.
Alleluia!

Let all creation praise the Lord!

Isaiah 35:1-7 (Message)

Wilderness and desert will sing joyously, the badlands will celebrate and
    flower—
Like the crocus in spring, bursting into blossom, a symphony of song and
    color.
Mountain glories of Lebanon—a gift.
Awesome Carmel, stunning Sharon—gifts.
God's resplendent glory, fully on display. God awesome, God majestic.
Energize the limp hands, strengthen the rubbery knees.
Tell fearful souls, "Courage! Take heart!
God is here, right here, on his way to put things right
And redress all wrongs. He's on his way! He'll save you!"
Blind eyes will be opened, deaf ears unstopped,
Lame men and women will leap like deer, the voiceless break into song.
Springs of water will burst out in the wilderness, streams flow in the
    desert.

Hot sands will become a cool oasis, thirsty ground a splashing fountain.
Even lowly jackals will have water to drink, and barren grasslands flourish richly.

Hallelujah, God will put all things right and redress all wrongs.

Romans 8:19-21 (Message)

I don't think there's any comparison between the present hard times and
the coming good times. The created world itself can hardly wait for what's
coming next. Everything in creation is being more or less held back. God
reins it in until both creation and all the creatures are ready and can be
released at the same moment into the glorious times ahead. Meanwhile,
the joyful anticipation deepens.

All around us we observe a pregnant creation. The difficult times of pain
throughout the world are simply birth pangs. But it's not only around us;
it's within us. The Spirit of God is arousing us within. We're also feeling
the birth pangs. These sterile and barren bodies of ours are yearning for
full deliverance. That is why waiting does not diminish us, any more than
waiting diminishes a pregnant mother. We are enlarged in the waiting.
We, of course, don't see what is enlarging us. But the longer we wait, the
larger we become, and the more joyful our expectancy.

**God, we believe all creation waits in anticipation for Christ's
return,**
When your creative power will transform all of life,
**And you will give birth to a resurrection world of fairness and
freedom.**
The difficult times of pain will be turned into songs of joy.
Scarcity will be transformed into abundance.
Greed will be replaced by generosity.
Oppression will be overcome by justice.
**God we believe that when your new world of wholeness and
shalom is born,**
Your healing power will be unleashed in its fullness;
The blind will see and the lame leap like deer.
Righteousness and faithfulness will reign,

The voiceless will break into song and streams will flow in the
desert.
All of creation will find its true purpose in Christ.

Our Father in heaven, hallowed be your name. Your Kingdom come, your will be done, on earth as in heaven. Give us
today our daily bread. Forgive us our sins, as we forgive those
who sin against us. Lead us not into temptation, but deliver
us from evil. For the kingdom, the power and the glory are
yours. Now and forever. Amen

Pause to offer specific prayers and thanksgivings.

Faithful God, creator of all times and seasons,
We so easily forget that hidden within the night's dark em-
brace are the seeds of life.
Remind us, loving God, that when all seems dark and empty,
You are still at work strengthening our roots, healing our
wounds, anchoring our lives.
Remind us, generous God, that when morning dawns,
It is the night's long rest that has sustained and nurtured our
souls.
Keep us, faithful God, through the dark journey of life,
So that when the new dawn breaks our roots may be deep and
strong.

Deep peace, pure white of the moon to you.
Deep peace, pure green of the grass to you.
Deep peace, pure brown of the earth to you.
Deep peace, pure grey of the dew to you.
Deep peace, pure blue of the sky to you.
Deep peace of the running wave to you.
Deep peace of the flowing air to you.
Deep peace of the quiet earth to you.
Deep peace of the shining stars to you.
Deep peace of the Son of peace to you forever.[13]

Deep peace of the God of life to you.
Deep peace of the Christ of love to you.
Deep peace of the Spirit of truth to you.
Deep peace of the God of Gods to you.
The peace of all peace be yours this night and forevermore,
Amen.

---

13. Prayer written by Fiona McLeod (1855-1905).

Tuesday

Christ and the Call to Love and Compassion

For a number of years I taught a course on incarnation and the urban poor for Fuller Theological Seminary in Seattle. I would often start the class by asking students, "What aspect of God's character do you most want to incarnate to the poor?" The first time I did this I was stunned by the answers. Judgment and punishment for sin predominated. Love was not even mentioned.

One of the most incomprehensible aspects of Christian faith is our belief that God cares deeply and passionately for humankind and as a result came into the world as a human child. Jesus came to be one of us to show us what God is really like. The God that we rejected and walked away from in the Garden has not walked away from us. Our loving God whose heart aches because of what this separation has done to us and the created world does not come seeking vengeance. Jesus, through his words and actions reveals the character of a caring, compassionate God who suffers through every agony we endure and who will do everything possible to restore the relationships that humankind has so grievously corrupted.

What kind of God do we want to incarnate to our world? Is it a God of love and compassion who leaves ninety nine sheep in order to rescue one that has gone astray, or One who constantly accuses those who do not follow God's ways? Is it a God who gets his hands dirty by entering, in a very personal and human way into the pain and suffering of our world or One who inflicts pain and anguish as punishment for our sins? Is it a God who celebrates life with enthusiasm by turning water into wine at a wedding or One who strips us of our joy by placing heavy burdens on our shoulders? Is it a God who hears our cries and brings justice for the poor and oppressed or One who stands aloof and indifferent to our pain?

For Christ, love of God was obviously intimately intertwined with love of neighbor and concern for the marginalized. God invites us to both extend Christ's love and compassion to others and also look and listen for where it is already revealed in the lives and faces of those around us. Living as Christ's representatives places tremendous responsibility on us. We cannot embody the presence of a loving God and still maintain our positions of privilege and power. If we believe we are meant to represent the image of a God of justice who is preferentially concerned for the poor it should impact all our actions. Incarnation must begin at the grassroots level. It influences decisions about the goods we buy, the places we invest our money and the ways we relate in our work place. It is reflected in our distress at the unjust wages paid to those at the bottom of the financial ladder, and our outrage at the emission of toxic waste into the environment. It is expressed in our concern for those we pass in the streets, especially the homeless, the drug addict, or the runaway teenager. It changes our attitudes towards those at work—our colleagues, our bosses, the cleaning staff and the message boy. And it revolutionizes our relationships to those we interact with in our home – not just our family but also our neighbors, the garbage collector and the postman.

Recognizing that we part of Christ's community also impacts how we interact with those who express their faith differently from us. As part of the body of Christ we are invited to worship with people of other cultures in peace and unity seeking to understand and respect their perspectives. We are invited to accept those who are different, to live and eat with them and to share our resources with them with no strings attached.

Focusing on the incarnational presence of Christ forces us to ask ourselves "How can Christ-in-me demonstrate his love and compassion through my actions today?" or "In what ways do the faces of my family, friends and those I pass in the street reflect the image of God?" Asking these questions has totally transformed my attitude towards work and my community. Reading the newspaper is no longer a way to gather information about the world, it is a doorway into prayer for those who are image bearers of the living God. Grocery shopping is no longer just to buy food, it is an opportunity to interact with people for whom God cares and Christ died.

Focusing Our Thoughts

Take a few minutes during the day to sit in silence and remember Christ's life and ministry. What aspects of Christ's life do you want to incarnate to the world?

- Reflect on the impact Christ's coming has had as he walked with you, comforted you and loved you at different stages of our life journey.

    1. Picture Christ walking with you in your childhood experiences.

    2. Picture Christ walking with you through your teenage struggles.

    3. Picture Christ walking with you as you make your adult decisions.

- Reflect on the faces of your family, friends, those you pass in the street or who live in poverty.

    1. Where have you seen Christ this week in friends and family, in the poor and the marginalized, in the sick and the dying, in people of other cultures and faiths?

    2. In what ways would you like to see the image of God more present in their faces?

- How does this impact your interactions with colleagues and friends?

- How does it motivate your relationships with your family?

- How does it motivate your contact with the marginalized in your community and around the world?

    1. Picture times during the day when you plan to pause and remind yourself of what it means to be Christ's incarnational presence to the world.

Focusing Our Prayers

- Pray for ways you could be God's incarnational presence to others.

- Pray for those in Christ's family who have been an incarnational example to you in your Christian walk

- Pray for those who seek to represent Christ in their daily work

  1. For those in the business community, service industry, educators and health care providers

  2. For those in government, police force, fire department, transportation industry

- Pray for those who seek to represent Christ through full time Christian ministry

  1. For your church and pastor and for all who serve Christ in the church

  2. For individuals and organizations that minister to the sick, the poor and the marginalized

- Pray for countries that need to see Christ's incarnational presence, particularly those torn apart by civil conflict or manmade disasters.

- Pray for people you know that need to see Christ's incarnational presence particularly for those with chronic or psychiatric illness, or injustice.

Morning Prayer

Jesus Christ, you are our God with a human face,
You are in charge of all creation yet you came and moved into
　　our neighborhood.
May this morning bring us word of your unfailing love.
Everything that is created gets its life from you,
Like this new day dawning, your life gives light to everyone,
May this morning bring us word of your unfailing love.
The day is new and fresh with promise,
It speaks of your unfailing love and faithfulness.
May this morning bring us word of your unfailing love.

> *Pause to reflect on what it means to be the bearer of
> Christ's love to the world.*

Jesus Christ, you are our God with a human face,
You entered human history as a child.
You came to be like us so that we might become like you.
You willingly walked our journey with us,
You were a friend of sinners, a companion to the poor.
You came to be like us so that we might become like you.
You laughed with us and celebrated our victories,
You wept with us and endured our pains.
You came to be like us so that we might become like you.
You walked beside us and shared our burdens,
You were a hater of injustice, a lover of children.
You came to be like us so that we might become like you.
You taught us what it really means to be human,
You challenged us to find life by giving it away.
You came to be like us so that we might become like you.
You showed us that living means dying to self,
And winning means losing our lives for others.
You came to be like us so that we might become like you.
Jesus Christ, our God with a human face,

Light of the world, reconciler of all peoples.
You came to be like us so that we might become like you.

Psalm 25:1-10 (NLT)

O LORD, I give my life to you. I trust in you, my God!
 Do not let me be disgraced,
   or let my enemies rejoice in my defeat.
No one who trusts in you will ever be disgraced,
   but disgrace comes to those who try to deceive others.
Show me the right path, O LORD;
   point out the road for me to follow.
Lead me by your truth and teach me,
   for you are the God who saves me.
 All day long I put my hope in you.
Remember, O LORD, your compassion and unfailing love,
   which you have shown from long ages past.
Do not remember the rebellious sins of my youth.
 Remember me in the light of your unfailing love,
    for you are merciful, O LORD.
The LORD is good and does what is right;
  he shows the proper path to those who go astray.
 He leads the humble in doing right, teaching them his way.
The LORD leads with unfailing love and faithfulness
  all who keep his covenant and obey his demands.

The Lord leads with unfailing love and faithfulness all who keep his covenant.

1 John 4:7-16 (Message)

My beloved friends, let us continue to love each other since love comes from God. Everyone who loves is born of God and experiences a relationship with God. The person who refuses to love doesn't know the first thing about God, because God is love—so you can't know him if you don't love. This is how God showed his love for us: God sent his only Son into the world so we might live through him. This is the kind of love we are talking about—not that we once upon a time loved God, but that he loved us and sent his Son as a sacrifice to clear away our sins and the damage they've done to our relationship with God.

My dear, dear friends, if God loved us like this, we certainly ought to love each other. No one has seen God, ever. But if we love one another, God dwells deeply within us, and his love becomes complete in us—perfect love!

This is how we know we're living steadily and deeply in him, and he in us: He's given us life from his life, from his very own Spirit. Also, we've seen for ourselves and continue to state openly that the Father sent his Son as Savior of the world. Everyone who confesses that Jesus is God's Son participates continuously in an intimate relationship with God. We know it so well, we've embraced it heart and soul, this love that comes from God.

Let us love one another since love comes from God.

Luke 4:16-21 (Message)

He came to Nazareth where he had been reared. As he always did on the Sabbath, he went to the meeting place. When he stood up to read, he was handed the scroll of the prophet Isaiah. Unrolling the scroll, he found the place where it was written, "God's Spirit is on me; he's chosen me to preach the Message of good news to the poor, Sent me to announce pardon to prisoners and recovery of sight to the blind, To set the burdened and battered free, to announce, "This is God's year to act!"

He rolled up the scroll, handed it back to the assistant, and sat down. Every eye in the place was on him, intent. Then he started in, "You've just heard Scripture make history. It came true just now in this place."

We believe in Jesus Christ, word made flesh,
Incarnate presence of God,
He came amongst us not in power, not in might, but as a child,
Born of a woman, raised as a refugee, servant of the poor
Lowly and humble he came,
Washing feet, embracing kids, touching outcasts
He came as a servant king
Loving, caring, compassionate he walked beside us
Shouldering our burdens, suffering our pain, healing our sicknesses,
He came as a God who hears our cries
Bringing freedom for the oppressed, justice for the poor

Providing food for the hungry, salvation for us all
He came as a God of celebration and joy
Sharing meals, celebrating feasts, laughing and rejoicing
He came to give us life
So that we might find life in doing his will.

Our Father in heaven, hallowed be your name. Your Kingdom come, your will be done, on earth as in heaven. Give us today our daily bread. Forgive us our sins, as we forgive those who sin against us. Lead us not into temptation, but deliver us from evil. For the kingdom, the power and the glory are yours. Now and forever. Amen

Pause to offer specific prayers and thanksgivings.

Jesus, you came into human history as an infant,
Come and protect all those who are vulnerable today.
God who came to live as one of us, hear our prayer.
You were born in a stable and lived with no home to call your own,
Come bring hope to all who are homeless today.
God who came to live as one of us, hear our prayer.
You fled into Egypt as a refugee and died a death of horrible violence,
Comfort all women and children who suffer the atrocities of war and flee conflict today.
God who came to live as one of us, hear our prayer.
Jesus, you were a friend of sinners and outcasts,
Befriend all who are ostracized because of illness, disability, race or gender today.
God who came to live as one of us, hear our prayer.
Jesus, you called the children to come to you so that you could bless them,
Welcome all the world's children, born and unborn, starving and well fed, abused and coddled.
God who came to live as one of us, hear our prayer.
Jesus, you touched the untouchable and cast out demons,

Heal all of us in whom the divine image is still hidden and distorted.
God who came to live as one of us, hear our prayer.

We rejoice this day because Jesus Christ has come into our world. May the joy of being part of a race in which God appeared in the flesh, overflow through our lives, in love and compassion to all those in whom the divine image is still hidden and distorted. May the brightness of Christ's light so shine in us, that it transforms the darkness of our broken world.

Christ who dwells among us,
Fill us this day with your presence,
Fill our lives with knowledge of your love,
Fill our thoughts with assurance of your salvation,
Fill our actions with willingness to serve,
Christ fill us with your presence,
So that we might fill others with your life.
Amen.

Evening Prayer

Jesus Christ, you are the light of the world,
Your light shines in the darkness and the darkness has not
    overcome it.
You are the One in whom we take refuge this night.
Jesus Christ, you are our strength and our rock,
You are our fortress and our deliverer,
You are the One in whom we take refuge this night.
Jesus Christ, we have set you always before us,
Because you are at our right hand we will not be shaken,
You are the One in whom we take refuge this night.
Jesus Christ, we praise you because you always counsel us,
Even when we are asleep you continue to instruct us,
You are the One in whom we take refuge this night.

Our hope is in the name of the Creator of life,
Our hope is in the name of the Christ of love,
Our hope is in the name of the Spirit of truth,
God, our hope comes from you.

> *Light a candle and reflect on where you have brought*
> *Christ's light into the world today.*

As this candle lights the darkness,
May your presence light our lives.
As its flame burns bright before us,
May your spirit burn bright within us.
As its warm glow surrounds us,
May the warmth of your love embrace us.

Christ as a light, illumine and guide us.
Christ as a shield, overshadow and cover us.
Christ be under us, Christ be over us.
Christ be beside us, on left and on right.
Christ be before us, Christ be behind us.

Christ be within us, Christ be without us.
Christ as a light, illumine and guide us.[14]

Psalm 121 (CEV)

I look to the hills. Where will I find help?
It will come from the Lord who created the heavens and the
  earth
The Lord is your protection
And he won't let you sleep or let you stumble
The protector of Israel doesn't doze or ever get drowsy
The Lord is your protector
There at your right side to shade you from the sun
You won't be harmed by the sun during the day or by the
  moon at night.
The Lord will protect you
And keep you safe from all dangers.
The Lord will protect you now and always wherever you go
The Lord will protect his people

Romans 8:33-39 (CEV)

If God says his chosen ones are acceptable to him, can anyone bring
charges against them? Or can anyone condemn them? No indeed! Christ
died and was raised to life, and now he is at God's right side, speaking
to him for us. Can anything separate us from the love of Christ? Can
trouble, suffering, and hard times, or hunger and nakedness, or danger
and death? It is exactly as the Scriptures say, "For you we face death all
day long. We are like sheep on their way to be butchered."

In everything we have won more than a victory because of Christ who
loves us. I am sure that nothing can separate us from God's love--not life
or death, not angels or spirits, not the present or the future, and not powers above or powers below. Nothing in all creation can separate us from
God's love for us in Christ Jesus our Lord!

Nothing in all creation can separate us from God's love.

---

14. Adapted from St. Patrick's Hymn by James C. Mangan (1803-1849).

John 1:14-20 (Message)

The Word became flesh and blood, and moved into the neighborhood. We saw the glory with our own eyes, the one-of-a-kind glory, like Father, like Son, generous inside and out, true from start to finish.

John pointed him out and called, "This is the One! The One I told you was coming after me but in fact was ahead of me. He has always been ahead of me, has always had the first word."

We all live off his generous bounty, gift after gift after gift. We got the basics from Moses, and then this exuberant giving and receiving, This endless knowing and understanding— all this came through Jesus, the Messiah. No one has ever seen God, not so much as a glimpse. This one-of-a-kind God-Expression, who exists at the very heart of the Father, has made him plain as day.

Praise God! The Word became flesh and moved into the neighborhood.

Jesus Christ, we believe that you are the human face of God,
You came to be like us so that we might become like you.
You cooked us food and washed our feet,
You embraced our kids and touched the outcasts.
Through your words and actions, you taught us what God is
    really like.
Jesus Christ, we believe that you became flesh and blood,
You moved into our neighborhood and freed us from our prisons,
You released those who were battered and judged their oppressors,
You took pity on the poor and fed those who were hungry.
Through your words and actions, you taught us what God is
    really like.
Jesus Christ, we believe you are the one-of-a-kind expression
    of God almighty.
You came in love and compassion to wipe away our tears,
You shouldered our burdens and healed our sick,
You heard our cries for help and took away our pain.

**Through your words and actions, you taught us what God is
really like.**
Jesus Christ, we believe that nothing can separate us from
your great love,
You came with laughter and joy, sharing our meals, celebrating
our feasts,
You encouraged our efforts and rejoiced at our successes,
Your loving friendship is everywhere present in our world.
**Through your words and actions, you taught us what God is
really like.**

**Our Father in heaven, hallowed be your name. Your King-
dom come, your will be done, on earth as in heaven. Give us
today our daily bread. Forgive us our sins, as we forgive those
who sin against us. Lead us not into temptation, but deliver
us from evil. For the kingdom, the power and the glory are
yours, now and forever. Amen.**

Pause to offer specific prayers and thanksgivings.

As this night descends, Christ be with us.
Be in our hearts and in our minds,
Be in our souls and in our spirits,
Be in our thoughts and in our dreams.
As the night descends, Christ be our friend and our companion.
Show us the love only you can give,
Show us the light only you can provide,
Show us the wholeness only you can reveal,
As this night descends, Christ surround us.
Circle us with your presence,
Keep protection near and danger far,
Bring us the assurance of your love.

The God of life with guarding hold you;
The loving Christ with guarding fold you;
The Holy Spirit, guarding mould you;

Each night of life to aid, enfold you;
Each day and night of life, uphold you.[15]

Christ our protector, guard us this night.
We commit our bodies, and our spirits into your hands.
Christ our companion, shield us this night fill us with your
    peace,
May your Cross keep us from harm and protect us as we
    sleep.
Christ our rescuer, bring us this night to the nearness of your
    love.

The peace of the Creator of joy be yours,
The peace of the Christ of hope be yours,
The peace of the Spirit of grace be yours,
The peace of the Father, the Son and the Holy Spirit be yours,
The peace of all peace be yours this night and evermore.
Amen.

---

15. The Northumbria Community Trust, *Celtic Daily Prayer* (New York: HarperCollins Publishers, 2002) 45.

Wednesday

The Holy Spirit and the Call to Unity

Every year in May I have the privilege of teaching a course on spiritual renewal for the Overseas Ministries Study Center in New Haven, Connecticut. The students come from around the world and include pastors and church leaders from Korea, Myanmar, Brazil, Kenya, Nigeria, and Tanzania, to name a few. It is an enriching but challenging experience as we struggle together to learn about God from our different cultural perspectives. Listening to the life journeys of my Asian, African, and Latin American brothers and sisters teaches me a lot about God and discipleship. This unique multicultural gathering reminds me of the outpouring of the Holy Spirit at Pentecost when the crowd exclaimed, "How is it that we each hear them in [our] own native language?" (Acts 2:9). One of the wonderful gifts of the Holy Spirit is that of understanding—understanding of ourselves, of God, and of our neighbors from other cultures and perspectives who look, think, and speak differently than we do.

God invites us to live into his resurrection-created world by very intentionally seeking to integrate our lives with God and God's ways. In order to do this we must constantly allow ourselves to be pushed outside the boundaries of our understanding. This is not something that comes naturally to any of us. In fact we cannot accomplish it without the infilling presence of the Holy Spirit. To be filled with the spirit means to consciously choose to lay down our own self-centered lives and the limited understanding of God that comes from our own cultural background. It means to deliberately seek to understand ourselves, God, and others in a way that enables us to live each moment more fully in God's presence and do God's will. This is a constant daily struggle as the Holy Spirit works to enlighten us. God's indwelling counselor both uncovers the hidden barriers that distort our ability to lead a life that is fully integrated with God and empowers us with God's gifts so that we can be more effective ambassadors of God's resurrection world.

There are many barriers that disconnect us from God and inhibit our understanding of God's ways. First, there are inner barriers: selfishness, covetousness, fear, feelings of inadequacy or abandonment, lack of trust, and our inability to accept God's love for us all separate us from God and God's life of wholeness. Other barriers destroy our intimacy with God. Busyness and the pressures of our 24/7 world, independence and the desire to do it our way all distort our ability to hear God's voice.

Still other barriers separate us from friends and neighbors near and far with whom God intends us to share life. Lack of forgiveness, fear of rejection, the desire to control, hostility to other opinions, greed, and refusal to listen to those with different viewpoints all separate us from friends, family, colleagues, people of other faiths and cultures with whom we share God's world.

There are also barriers that separate us from God's creation. Polluting, consumer-driven lifestyles, disregard for God's stewardship principles, and lack of respect for God's creation all distance us from the God revealed in the created world.

God's indwelling Spirit is constantly at work breaking down these barriers and drawing us closer to a life that is fully integrated with God and God's purposes.

Focusing Our Thoughts

Take a few minutes during the day to reflect on the ongoing work of the Holy Spirit.

* Remind yourself of God's spirit at work in your life and the world around you:

  1. Begin with silence allowing the Spirit to speak to you.

  2. Thank God for specific occasions in the past when you were aware of God's Spirit working within you, convicting, transforming, and bringing you wholeness.

  3. Thank God for times when God has worked through you to encourage others in their journey towards wholeness.

* Remind yourself of God's call on your life[16]:

  1. How could you more effectively live into this calling?

  2. What hidden parts of your life does God want to move towards wholeness so that you can more authentically represent God's resurrection-created world?

  3. What gifts has the Holy Spirit anointed you with that could equip others for the good works God has prepared for all of us to do?

* How could you more effectively use your gifts to model God's resurrection-created world?

* Picture times throughout the day when you plan to pause and remind yourself of God's indwelling spirit.

---

16. If you do not have a clear sense of God's call on your life, see Christine and Tom Sine, *Living on Purpose: How to Find God's Best For your Life* (Baker Books, 2002) for an active listening process that will enable you to develop a calling statement.

Focusing Our Prayers

- Pray for a fresh touch of God's Spirit in your own life.

  1. For wisdom, discernment and the ability to learn from the great counselor in the day's challenges.

  2. For God's comfort and compassion in your interaction with others.

  3. For guidance in your own vocational call and all your daily activities.

- Pray for specific situations in which you are aware of the Holy Spirit at work in the church and the world.

- Pray for people of other faiths that the One who leads us into all truth may work in their lives.

- Pray for unsaved friends and acquaintances that God's Spirit may lead them into all truth.

Morning Prayer

God, who enables us to stand firm in Christ,
Has placed the Holy Spirit in our hearts.
The seal of God's ownership is on us,
A deposit guaranteeing what is to come.
God, your Spirit fills us and draws us into your resurrection
world,
May we lay down our own self-centered lives this day.
May we consciously live each moment,
Seeking to be in your presence and doing your will.

Pause to invite the Holy Spirit into your day's activities.

God, your spirit fell like tongues of fire.
It filled those that were empty,
It empowered those that were weary.
God, your spirit fell like tongues of fire.
It brought together those that were divided,
It reassured those who were afraid.
God, your spirit still falls like tongues of fire.
By its power we can walk together as one,
By its power we can find strength to share.
God, your spirit still falls like tongues of fire.
By its power we can find freedom in loving each other,
By its power we can find life in you.
God, your spirit still falls like tongues of fire.

1 Corinthians 12:1-11 (Message)

What I want to talk about now is the various ways God's Spirit gets worked into our lives. This is complex and often misunderstood, but I want you to be informed and knowledgeable. Remember how you were when you didn't know God, led from one phony god to another, never knowing what you were doing, just doing it because everybody else did it? It's different in this life. God wants us to use our intelligence, to seek to understand as well as we can. For instance, by using your heads, you know perfectly well that the Spirit of God would never prompt anyone to say "Jesus be damned!" Nor would anyone be inclined to say "Jesus is Master!" without the insight of the Holy Spirit.

God's various gifts are handed out everywhere; but they all originate in God's Spirit. God's various ministries are carried out everywhere; but they all originate in God's Spirit. God's various expressions of power are in action everywhere; but God himself is behind it all. Each person is given something to do that shows who God is: Everyone gets in on it, everyone benefits. All kinds of things are handed out by the Spirit, and to all kinds of people! The variety is wonderful: wise counsel, clear understanding, simple trust, healing the sick, miraculous acts, proclamation, distinguishing between spirits, tongues, interpretation of tongues. All these gifts have a common origin, but are handed out one by one by the one Spirit of God. He decides who gets what, and when.

Praise God for the gifts of the Spirit.

Galatians 5:1, 13-26 (CEV)

Christ has set us free! This means we are really free. Now hold on to your freedom and don't ever become slaves of the Law again. My friends, you were chosen to be free. So don't use your freedom as an excuse to do anything you want. Use it as an opportunity to serve each other with love. All that the Law says can be summed up in the command to love others as much as you love yourself. But if you keep attacking each other like wild animals, you had better watch out or you will destroy yourselves. If you are guided by the Spirit, you won't obey your selfish desires. The Spirit and your desires are enemies of each other. They are always fighting each other and keeping you from doing what you feel you should. But if you obey the Spirit, the Law of Moses has no control over you. People's desires make them give in to immoral ways, filthy thoughts, and shameful deeds. They worship idols, practice witchcraft, hate others, and are hard to get along with. People become jealous, angry, and selfish. They not only argue and cause trouble, but they are envious. They get drunk, carry on at wild parties, and do other evil things as well. I told you before, and I am telling you again: No one who does these things will share in the blessings of God's kingdom. God's Spirit makes us loving, happy, peaceful, patient, kind, good, faithful, gentle, and self-controlled. There is no law against behaving in any of these ways. And because we belong to

Christ Jesus, we have killed our selfish feelings and desires. God's Spirit has given us life, and so we should follow the Spirit. But don't be conceited or make others jealous by claiming to be better than they are.

Hallelujah, God's spirit sets us free!

John 14:15-21 (CEV)

Jesus said to his disciples: "If you love me, you will do as I command. Then I will ask the Father to send you the Holy Spirit who will help you and always be with you. The Spirit will show you what is true. The people of this world cannot accept the Spirit, because they don't see or know him. But you know the Spirit, who is with you and will keep on living in you. I won't leave you like orphans. I will come back to you. In a little while the people of this world won't be able to see me, but you will see me. And because I live, you will live. Then you will know that I am one with the Father. You will know that you are one with me, and I am one with you. If you love me, you will do what I have said, and my Father will love you. I will also love you and show you what I am like."

Thank God! God's Spirit will show us what is true.

God, we believe you sent your Spirit to live within us,
To draw us into the freedom of your resurrection world
Your indwelling Spirit leads us into all truth.
God, we believe your Spirit breaks down the barriers that
   imprison us,
Filling us with the values of your kingdom of love.
**Your comforting Spirit encourages us to worship God with all
   our hearts.**
God, we believe your Spirit develops the talents you have
   placed within us,
Enabling us to serve others in compassion and love.
Your empowering Spirit equips us with gifts for service.
God, we believe your Spirit writes your law of love on our
   hearts,
Transforming our self-centeredness into concern for others.
**Your liberating Spirit sets us free to love our neighbors as we
   do ourselves.**

God, we believe your Spirit calls us to follow you,
Laying down all that distracts us from a wholehearted commit-
ment to your ways.
God, we believe this is the path from death to eternal life.

**Our Father in heaven, hallowed be your name. Your King-
dom come, your will be done, on earth as in heaven. Give us
today our daily bread. Forgive us our sins, as we forgive those
who sin against us. Lead us not into temptation, but deliver
us from evil. For the kingdom, the power and the glory are
yours, now and forever. Amen.**

Pause to offer specific prayers and thanksgivings.

God, thank you for your spirit breaking down barriers within
and without,
Barriers that distort our ability to lead a life fully integrated
with you and your ways,
Forgive us for the times we have deliberately resisted the
Spirit's work,
Life-giving spirit, God's advocate and guide, have mercy on us.
Forgive us, God, for the barriers we create in ourselves,
Barriers that resist your healing work and prevent us moving
toward wholeness,
Forgive our self-centeredness, our anger, our fear of change,
our lack of trust in your love.
Life-giving spirit, God's advocate and guide, have mercy on us.
Forgive us, God, for barriers we create between us and you,
Barriers that separate us from your love and the assurance of
your salvation,
Forgive our busyness, our independence, our desire to go our
own way.
Life-giving spirit, God's advocate and guide, have mercy on us.
Forgive us, God, for the barriers we create between us and
each other,
Barriers that separate us from neighbors near and far and
inhibit mutual love and care,

Forgive our resentment of others, our love of control, our indifference to the poor.
Life-giving spirit, God's advocate and guide, have mercy on us.
Forgive us, God, for the barriers we create between us and your beautiful creation,
Barriers that abuse your world and deny our responsibility as stewards,
Forgive our greed, our misuse of resources, our pollution of the environment.
Life-giving spirit, God's advocate and guide, have mercy on us.
God, by the power of your spirit, free us and break down these barriers,
Turn us away from the bondage of a life lived for ourselves and our own desires,
May your spirit guide us into the freedom of life lived for you and your purposes.
Life-giving spirit, God's advocate and guide, have mercy on us.

Glorious God and Father of our Lord Jesus Christ,
We go into this day knowing your Spirit dwells in us.
May your Counselor make us wise and help us understand what it means to know you.
May the Spirit's fire ignite our hearts so that we understand the hope of being chosen by God.
May we discover the glorious blessings we share together with all God's people.

God, we go into this day
Knowing it is you who makes us stand firm in Christ.
We are filled with your Spirit,
We are anointed to serve,
We go out to bring resurrection life.

May the grace of the Lord Jesus Christ, the love of God and the fellowship of the Holy Spirit be with you all, this day and forever.
Amen

Evening Prayer

God almighty, your spirit is with us.
You alone grant us sleep and make us dwell in safety,
May we lie down this night and rest in peace.

We place our lives in your safe keeping this night, O God.
We place them in your keeping, O Jesus Christ.
We place them in your keeping, O Holy Spirit.
The Three who would defend and shelter all,
Be keeping us this night from harm.[19]

> *Silence for lighting of the candle. Pause to remind your-*
> *self of the ongoing work of the Spirit.*

God, the light of the Spirit has shined today,
Like tongues of fire that have renewed and restored.
In our rising and our sleeping,
In our working and our playing,
In our joys and in our sorrows,
Your Spirit's brightness has dispelled the darkness.
In our loving and caring,
In our touching and our listening,
In our thoughts and in our actions,
God's Spirit has brought life out of death.

Psalm 146 (CEV)

God, we will shout your praises as long as we live.
With all that I am I will shout his praises.
I will sing and praise the Lord God for as long as I live.
You can't depend on anyone, not even on a great leader.
Once they die and are buried, that will be the end of all their
   plans.

---

18. Adapted from Northumbria Community Trust, *Celtic Daily Prayer*
(New York: HarperCollins Publishers, 2002), 42.

The Lord God of Jacob blesses everyone who trusts in him and
depends on him.
God made heaven and earth, he created the sea and every-
thing else. God always keeps his word.
He gives justice to the poor and food to the hungry
The Lord sets prisoners free and heals blind eyes
He gives a helping hand to everyone who falls
The Lord loves good people and looks after strangers.
He defends the rights of orphans and widows, but destroys the
wicked
The Lord God of Zion will rule forever!
God, we will shout your praises as long as we live.

Ephesians 3:14 – 4:6 (NLT)

When I think of all this, I fall to my knees and pray to the Father, the
Creator of everything in heaven and on earth. I pray that from his
glorious, unlimited resources he will empower you with inner strength
through his Spirit. Then Christ will make his home in your hearts as you
trust in him. Your roots will grow down into God's love and keep you
strong. And may you have the power to understand, as all God's people
should, how wide, how long, how high, and how deep his love is. May
you experience the love of Christ, though it is too great to understand
fully. Then you will be made complete with all the fullness of life and
power that comes from God. Now all glory to God, who is able, through
his mighty power at work within us, to accomplish infinitely more than
we might ask or think. Glory to him in the church and in Christ Jesus
through all generations forever and ever! Amen.

Therefore I, a prisoner for serving the Lord, beg you to lead a life worthy
of your calling, for you have been called by God. Always be humble and
gentle. Be patient with each other, making allowance for each other's
faults because of your love. Make every effort to keep yourselves united
in the Spirit, binding yourselves together with peace. For there is one
body and one Spirit, just as you have been called to one glorious hope for
the future. There is one Lord, one faith, one baptism, and one God and
Father, who is over all and in all and living through all.

May we live a life that is worthy of God.

John 14:23-27 (NLT)

Jesus replied, "All who love me will do what I say. My Father will love them, and we will come and make our home with each of them. Anyone who doesn't love me will not obey me. And remember, my words are not my own. What I am telling you is from the Father who sent me. I am telling you these things now while I am still with you. But when the Father sends the Advocate as my representative—that is, the Holy Spirit—he will teach you everything and will remind you of everything I have told you. "I am leaving you with a gift—peace of mind and heart. And the peace I give is a gift the world cannot give. So don't be troubled or afraid.

The Apostles Creed (Modern English Version)[19]

I believe in God, the Father almighty,
  creator of heaven and earth.
I believe in Jesus Christ, God's only Son, our Lord,
  who was conceived by the Holy Spirit,
  born of the Virgin Mary,
  suffered under Pontius Pilate,
  was crucified, died, and was buried;
  he descended to the dead.
On the third day he rose again;
  he ascended into heaven,
  he is seated at the right hand of the Father,
  and he will come again to judge the living and the dead.
I believe in the Holy Spirit,
  the holy catholic church,
  the communion of saints,

---

19. The Apostles' Creed, or *Symbolum Apostolorum*, is the most popular creed used by Western Christians. Its central doctrines are the Trinity and God the Creator. Legend has it that it was written by the Apostles after Christ ascended into heaven. Though this is not true, the name stuck. The earliest written version is the *Interrogatory Creed of Hippolytus* (ca. 215 AD). The current form is first found in the writings of Caesarius of Arles (d. 542).

the forgiveness of sins,
 the resurrection of the body,
 and the life everlasting. Amen.

Our Father in heaven, hallowed be your name. Your Kingdom come, your will be done, on earth as in heaven. Give us today our daily bread. Forgive us our sins, as we forgive those who sin against us. Lead us not into temptation, but deliver us from evil. For the kingdom, the power and the glory are yours, now and forever. Amen.

God, you fill us with your spirit
So that we can hear your voice.
You ask us to listen
So that we can know your ways.
You send us out to serve
So that we can be your people.
Come down, Father of life,
Fill us with your love.
Come in, Christ of peace,
Anoint us with compassion.
Come amongst us, Spirit of joy,
Teach us to celebrate your ways.

Spirit of God, encircle us this night,
Assure us of your presence.
Breath of life, refresh us,
Strengthen our gifts for your service.
Indwelling seal of God, guide us,
Increase our concern for God's broken people.
Bringer of truth, dream in us,
Grant us glimpses of God's new world.

The peace of all peace be yours this night
In the name of the Father, and of the Son
And of the Holy Spirit,
Amen.

Thursday

Community: Celebrating Life Together

My husband Tom and I live in a small intentional community in Seattle called the Mustard Seed House. We inhabit the middle floor of a triplex with a family in the apartment above and a couple in the basement apartment below. We say morning prayers daily, share meals at least once a week, and garden together once a month. We love hospitality and enjoy entertaining guests from around the world. We find that sharing life together in this way is an enriching experience. We can support each other through times of struggle and encourage each other in our spiritual disciplines and life decisions. Even our conflicts become opportunities to learn more about God and each other.

I have lived in community most of my adult life and am convinced that it is impossible to stand against the pressures of our individualistic, consumer-driven culture alone. It is only in community together that we find the support and accountability we need to follow Christ on a daily basis.

Early Christians believed that God comes to us in community—Father, Son, and Holy Spirit—a perfect harmony of relationship. They reasoned that since the essential nature of God is love, and because it is impossible to practice love in isolation, God the Trinity must be a model of perfect community.

To become a disciple meant to be drawn into this community of mutual love and perfect relationship—not alone, but as part of God's family with sisters and brothers from every tribe and nation, with the rich and the poor, the young and the old, the sick, the lonely, the disabled, the homeless, the marginalized, and the abandoned. If God comes to us in community, then it is impossible to reflect the image of God unless we too are willing to share life with others in God's community. Alone, we are a very poor reflection of God. It is only as we come together in unity, love, and mutual concern that we have any hope of truly reflecting the image of the loving God of the universe, who draws us into a community not of uniformity, but of diversity. Once we recognize we are part of the same family—God's family—we can willingly share life together with others.

To share life as God intends encourages us to willingly enter into the life journeys of brothers and sisters from around the world. That means walking alongside people from other cultures and perspectives, learning to understand their viewpoints, being willing to share their burdens, embrace their pain, and do what we can to alleviate their suffering. We are called to show God's love by sharing our talents and resources to enable others to enter into the freedoms of Christ's kingdom.

Probably most challenging of all, we must be willing to share our journey with sisters and brothers who have been marginalized within our own communities. We need to learn to accept and embrace them as persons made in the image of God and look not for where that image is damaged and scarred, but rather for where it shines through as the person God intended them to be. We should willingly walk alongside the homeless, the disabled, and the despised and give them the freedom to challenge and question our viewpoints. We must learn to be vulnerable and share our own pain, struggles, and heartaches. Then we must allow them to reach into our lives and lead us into the freedom of God's shalom world.

Focusing Our Thoughts

Set aside a few minutes during the day to remind yourself of God's wonderfully diverse international community of which you are a part:

- Thank God for the richness of your faith that has grown through the experiences and witness of people from other cultures.

- Remind yourself of those from other cultures and faiths who have impacted your life.

  1. What opportunities continue to provide meaningful interaction with people of other faiths and cultures?

- Focus your life on God's community and the need for unity and understanding:

  1. Remind yourself of those people and communities that have been influential in your life.

  2. Thank God for those with whom you experience community.

  3. Remind yourself of those you are aware of who are excluded from community because of race, culture, social strata, or disability?

- How could you help your community to embrace them more?

  1. Remind yourself of areas in your life where you need to see restoration of community and relationship.

  2. In what ways have you helped to build community in your neighborhood, local community, or around the world?

- Picture times throughout the day when you plan to pause and remind yourself of God's international family.

Focusing Our Prayers

- Pray for people who live and work in your local community:
  1. For shop keepers, bankers, bus drivers, service station attendants, garbage collectors, and postal workers.
  2. For urban planners, council members, emergency workers, and police.
  3. For those who serve the poor, the sick, and the vulnerable.

- Pray for the unity of God's people around the world:
  1. For the unity of all Christians from every nation and creed.
  2. For those in the church that work for reconciliation and peace between peoples and faiths.
  3. For your own church community and its unity with other local churches.

- Pray for those you know who are involved in community restoration:
  1. For those who work in community development globally or locally.
  2. For ministries that work for reconciliation and restoration within local and global communities.

- Pray for those in God's community who:
  1. Suffer from AIDS, malaria, and other debilitating illnesses.
  2. Face persecution or death because of their faith.
  3. Are discriminated against because of race, age, social strata, or gender.

- Pray for those who seek to authentically live as God's kingdom communities.

Morning Prayer

Let us gather with God's faithful followers from every tribe and
nation,
With people of every language and culture to worship God
revealed in Jesus Christ.
**We gather together with sisters and brothers from every
tribe and nation and culture.**
**We want to share life together as members of God's eternal
family.**
Sharing life as sisters and brothers means entering into the
joys and sorrows of others.
We join with those in Africa, Asia, the Americas, Europe, Australia, and the many islands.
**God, you offer us wholeness, not alone, but as part of your
redeemed community.**
**We want to share life together as members of your eternal
family.**
We are called to love others and to be more concerned for
their needs than for our own,
Yet often we focus on ourselves, greedily holding onto what
you intend us to share.
**God, renew our hearts and minds so that we will want to
share life with all your eternal family.**
**May we, in word and deed, be your witnesses of love and
unity in the world.**

God who created us is with us,
And with our brothers and sisters from every tribe and nation.
Christ who saved us is with us,
And with our brothers and sisters from every tribe and nation.
The Holy Spirit who brings us unity is with us,
And with our brothers and sisters from every tribe and nation.

Pause to remind yourself of God's worldwide community.

This world we live in, this town we live in,
This street we live in, this house we live in,
May each be the focus of our prayer.
Those we live with, those we rub shoulders with,
Those we work with, those we don't get on with,
May each be the focus of our prayer.
Those who laugh, those who cry,
Those who hurt, those who hide,
May each be the focus of our prayer.
Prayer centered less on self, and more on others,
Less on our circumstances, more on the needs of others,
May this be the focus of our prayer.
May our lives be likewise centered, less on self and more on
    God,
And through God to the world in which we live and move,
May these be the focus of our prayer.[20]

Psalm 67 (CEV)

Our God, be kind and bless us! Be pleased and smile.
Then everyone on earth will learn to follow you,
And all nations will see your power to save us.
Make everyone praise you and shout your praises.
Let the nations celebrate with joyful songs,
because you judge fairly and guide all nations.
Make everyone praise you and shout your praises.
Our God has blessed the earth with a wonderful harvest!
Pray for his blessings to continue and for everyone on earth to worship
our God.

**May all the nations praise God and celebrate with joyful
songs.**

---

20. John Birch, accessed at http://www.faithandworship.com/prayers_
world.html. Used with permission.

Isaiah 2:1-4 (Message)

This is the message that I was given about Judah and Jerusalem: In the future, the mountain with the Lord's temple will be the highest of all. It will reach above the hills; every nation will rush to it. Many people will come and say, "Let's go to the mountain of the LORD God of Jacob and worship in his temple." The Lord will teach us his Law from Jerusalem, and we will obey him. He will settle arguments between nations. They will pound their swords and their spears into rakes and shovels; they will never make war or attack one another.

Praise God there will never be war or injustice again.

Luke 10:25-38 (Message)

Just then a religion scholar stood up with a question to test Jesus. "Teacher, what do I need to do to get eternal life?" He answered, "What's written in God's Law? How do you interpret it?" He said, "That you love the Lord your God with all your passion and prayer and muscle and intelligence—and that you love your neighbor as well as you do yourself." "Good answer!" said Jesus. "Do it and you'll live."

Looking for a loophole, he asked, "And how do you define 'neighbor'?"

Jesus answered by telling a story. "There was once a man traveling from Jerusalem to Jericho. On the way he was attacked by robbers. They took his clothes, beat him up, and went off leaving him half-dead. Luckily, a priest was on his way down the same road, but when he saw him he angled across to the other side. Then a Levite religious man showed up; he also avoided the injured man. A Samaritan traveling the road came on him. When he saw the man's condition, his heart went out to him. He gave him first aid, disinfecting and bandaging his wounds. Then he lifted him onto his donkey, led him to an inn, and made him comfortable. In the morning he took out two silver coins and gave them to the innkeeper, saying, 'Take good care of him. If it costs any more, put it on my bill—I'll pay you on my way back.'

"What do you think? Which of the three became a neighbor to the man attacked by robbers?"

"The one who treated him kindly," the religion scholar responded.

Jesus said, "Go and do the same."

We believe and trust in God the creator,
Who made us to be neighbors together,
Brothers and sisters from every tribe and nation and culture.
We believe and trust in Christ the redeemer,
Who saves us from self-centeredness and isolation,
To be joined together as parts of a body,
That loves and cares for each other.
We believe and trust in the Holy Spirit our enabler,
Who calls us to be one family,
With the rich, the poor, the disabled and the whole.
With the young, the old, the oppressed and despised.
We believe and trust in God,
Who welcomes us home into the eternal world,
Where justice and love will reign forever.
We believe and trust in God's new world coming,
Where one day together with sisters and brothers from all
    nations,
We will be healed and made whole to become all that God
    intends us to be.

Our Father in heaven, hallowed be your name. Your Kingdom come, your will be done, on earth as in heaven. Give us
today our daily bread. Forgive us our sins, as we forgive those
who sin against us. Lead us not into temptation, but deliver
us from evil. For the kingdom, the power and the glory are
yours, now and forever. Amen

Pause to offer specific prayers and thanksgivings.

God, your world is broken and in pain,
Broken by hunger that kills our brothers and sisters,
Broken by injustice that enslaves and oppresses our friends,
Broken by disease that deprives us of our loved ones.
Forgive us for our complicity, for when we were indifferent to
    cries of anguish,
Forgive us for acts that have polluted and destroyed immu-
    nity,

Forgive us for the times we could have shared our food,
Forgive us for places we should have spoken out.
Cleanse our hearts and wash away our sins,
Fill us with your peace and restore our joy in your salvation,
May we willingly count the cost of our responsibility to our neighbors near and far,
May we willingly enter into your community of peace and justice.

God, we want to share life together,
Break down the barriers dividing us from our brothers and sisters around the world.
Lord, have mercy.
God, we want to share life together,
Move us beyond our prejudices to live in unity and peace with those who are different.
Lord, have mercy.
God, we want to share life together,
Open our minds to appreciate our differences and come to mutual understanding.
Lord, have mercy.
Where there is war may we bring glimpses of peace,
And share life with all who are torn apart by violence, oppression, and dissension.
Christ, have mercy.
Where there is despair may we bring the promise of hope,
And share life with all who live in poverty, sickness, and injustice.
Christ, have mercy.
Where there is hate may we be instruments of God's love,
And share life with all who are divided by race, culture, disabilities, or gender.
Christ, have mercy.
God, we want to share life together,
Unite us in that great community of sisters and brothers from every nation that is Christ's body.

Lord, have mercy.
God, we want to share life together,
Bind us together with the love, peace, mutual concern, and
    cultural diversity that represent you.
Lord, have mercy.
God, we want to share life together,
One family living and serving together under the lordship of
    Christ and in the fellowship of the Holy Spirit.
Lord, have mercy.

O Lord our God, listen to us in this place.
Accept also the prayers of our sisters and brothers,
Those in Africa, Asia, Australia, the Americas, Europe, the
    Middle East, and the many islands of our planet.
We are all one in prayer,
So may we, as one, rightly carry out your commission.
May we witness to your love and share life in unity and har-
    mony,
In the church and around the world.
Accept all our prayers graciously,
Those in our words, and those in the language of others.
They are offered in Jesus' name.[21]
Amen

---

21. Adapted from a Ghanaian prayer.

Evening Prayer

God who comes to us in community,
Come to us this night.
Unite us with your Spirit.
Welcome us to your banquet table,
Include us in your eternal family,
Make us one in you.

> Pause to remind yourself of God the Trinity who comes
> to us as a perfect community of relationship.

God of infinite love, you come,
Father, Son, and Holy Spirit,
Perfect relationship, perfect community.
Creator, Redeemer, Sustainer, you come,
The three in one, the one in three.
You come to offer us community,
Mothers and daughters, fathers and sons.
Male and female, oppressed and free, disabled and whole,
You invite us into your community.
That together we might grow spiritually,
And become mature in Jesus Christ.
We need your community,
To keep us accountable to your call,
For we are called to serve one another.
We need your community,
To equip and develop your Holy Spirit gifts,
So that we can build one another up.
We need your community,
For prayer and encouragement,
For fellowship and festivity, for worship of you.
We need your community,
To witness to your all-inclusive love,
For only in community are we made whole.
One people together, family of the living God.

Psalm 133 (Message)

How wonderful, how beautiful, when brothers and sisters get along!
  It's like costly anointing oil
    flowing down head and beard,
  Flowing down Aaron's beard,
    flowing down the collar of his priestly robes.
  It's like the dew on Mount Hermon
    flowing down the slopes of Zion.
  Yes, that's where GOD commands the blessing,
    ordains eternal life.

Adapted from Isaiah 25:1-10 (Message)

Almighty God, you have already done your share of miracle-wonders,
You changed water into wine at a wedding,
And multiplied the fish and loaves to feed thousands.
All-knowing God, your well-laid plans are solid and sure.
One day superpowers will see them and honor you,
Brutal oppressors will bow in worshipful reverence.
All-caring God, one day all humanity will see you care for poor people in trouble.
You will provide a warm, dry place in bad weather and a cool place in the heat,
You will shelter all your people from the storm and shade them from the sun,
All-loving God, on your holy mountain you will wipe the tears from every face.
You will strip away the grave clothes that cover all nations,
You will remove every sign of disgrace from your people wherever they are.
All-powerful God, on your mountain you will banish the power of death forever.
There you will throw a feast for all the people of the world,
A feast of the finest foods with lavish desserts and vintage wines,

All-providing God, one day your mountain will rise above all others.

Yes! God, you say so! Yes, you are our God, the one we waited for!

We waited and hoped for God. Now you are here and have welcomed us to your feast.

Let's celebrate and sing the joy of God's salvation; God's hand rests on this holy mountain!

Acts 4:33-36 (Message)

The whole congregation of believers was united as one—one heart, one mind! They didn't even claim ownership of their own possessions. No one said, "That's mine; you can't have it." They shared everything. The apostles gave powerful witness to the resurrection of the Master Jesus, and grace was on all of them.

And so it turned out that not a person among them was needy. Those who owned fields or houses sold them and brought the price of the sale to the apostles and made an offering of it. The apostles then distributed it according to each person's need.

Luke 14:16-24 (Message)

"For there was once a man who threw a great dinner party and invited many. When it was time for dinner, he sent out his servant to the invited guests, saying, 'Come on in; the food's on the table.'

"Then they all began to beg off, one after another making excuses. The first said, 'I bought a piece of property and need to look it over. Send my regrets.' Another said, 'I just bought five teams of oxen, and I really need to check them out. Send my regrets.' And yet another said, 'I just got married and need to get home to my wife.'

"The servant went back and told the master what had happened. He was outraged and told the servant, 'Quickly, get out into the city streets and alleys. Collect all who look like they need a square meal, all the misfits and homeless and wretched you can lay your hands on, and bring them here.' The servant reported back, 'Master, I did what you commanded— and there's still room.'

"The master said, 'Then go to the country roads. Whoever you find, drag them in. I want my house full! Let me tell you, not one of those originally invited is going to get so much as a bite at my dinner party.'"

Lord Jesus Christ, we believe you welcome us all to your banquet table.
May we open our arms to embrace you,
May we see you in the face of a stranger,
May we welcome you in the love of a friend.
We believe you welcome the abandoned, the misfit, the wretched to your feast.
Forgive us for the times we have allowed our prejudices to overrule,
And rejected you because you were different, ostracized, or despised.
We believe that there is beauty hidden in each person,
Forgive us for the times we have failed to see your face,
Because you are disabled, poor, or homeless.
We believe we are all precious in your sight.
Forgive us for when we counted you unworthy of our love,
For when we have been indifferent to your cries.
We believe we are called to share life together as members of one family,
Forgive us for when we were unconcerned for your suffering,
And failed to see others in your community as you do.
We are all created in God's image,
Redeemed by Christ,
Filled with the Holy Spirit.
We are all invited to feast at God's banquet table.
We are welcomed into God's eternal kingdom,
With all the peoples' of the earth.

Our Father in heaven, hallowed be your name. Your Kingdom come, your will be done, on earth as in heaven. Give us today our daily bread. Forgive us our sins, as we forgive those who sin against us. Lead us not into temptation, but deliver

**us from evil. For the kingdom, the power and the glory are
yours, now and forever. Amen**

Pause to offer specific prayers and thanksgivings.

Brigit's Feast[22]

I should like a great lake of finest ale,
For the King of Kings.
I should like a table of the choicest food,
For the family of heaven.
Let the ale be made from the fruits of faith,
And the food be forgiving love.
**I should welcome the poor to my feast,
For they are God's children.
I should welcome the sick to my feast,
For they are God's joy.
Let the poor sit with Jesus at the highest place,
And the sick dance with the angels.**
God bless the poor,
God bless the sick,
And bless our human race.
**God bless our food,
God bless our drink,
All homes, O God, embrace.**

God, all-powerful and all-knowing, encircle your community,
Keep love within and fear without,
Keep peace within and violence out.
Circle us with your presence.
God, all-loving and all-embracing, encircle your community,
Keep wholeness in and disease without,
Keep care within and selfishness out.

---

22. Ancient Celtic prayer attributed to St. Brigit of Kildare (ca. 451-525 AD).

Circle us with your love.
God, all-mighty and all-caring, encircle your community,
Keep truth within and injustice out,
Keep acceptance in and prejudice out.
Circle us with your peace.

The blessing of God be upon you this night,
The blessing of the God of community.
The blessing of Christ be upon you,
The blessing of the Christ of love.
The blessing of the spirit be upon you,
The blessing of the spirit of peace.
The blessing of the God of gods be upon you,
The blessing of the God of life be yours this night and forever.
Amen

Friday

Crucifixion and the Way of the Cross

I love to collect photos of art that portray the gospel story and have a huge array of images of the cross of Christ, depicting what is probably the most commonly painted event in history. Some portray the crucifixion by vividly expressing the pain and agony Christ must have endured in his final moments. Others portray the resurrection—empty crosses that invite us into the hope and joy of the risen Christ and the wonder of God's resurrection-created world.

At the center of God's new world is not a throne but a cross. In fact, this cross with its promise of transformed lives and a renewed world does indeed stand at the very center not just of human history, but of life itself. The good news of the gospel is that Christ's cross is not primarily a symbol of pain and suffering or of the sinfulness of humankind. What the Romans intended as an implement of oppression and torture became a symbol of freedom and hope. It highlights the love of a God who cares for us so passionately, so deeply that he allowed his son to suffer and die to bring us freedom.

To fully appreciate God's redemptive work we must remember that for there to be new life there must first be death. For there to be resurrection there must first be crucifixion. For the joy that was set before him—the joy of opening a doorway into the wholeness and love of God's eternal world—Jesus Christ willingly endured the cross. At the cross, pain and healing embraced as Christ took into himself all the pain and agony that human beings have inflicted on themselves, on each other, and on creation and transformed it into wholeness and joy. At the cross, all that was broken and corrupted at the fall is restored and made new.

Repentance involves far more than forgiveness for a bad conscience or a turning away from bad habits. It requires a restructuring of our scale of values and a reorientation of our personalities. It beckons us to lay down the weapons of rebellion against God and accept the Cross of Christ as death to the world so that we can live before God. Jesus Christ does not rule like any earthly king however. He does not rule through power and privilege or through military might and oppression, but through service and humility. To walk as his disciple means to walk with this same humility—being willing to give up our own desires and ambitions and to become a servant as he did, identifying with those who are hungry, oppressed, or separated from God. For the joy that is set before us—the joy of participating in the in-breaking of God's new world—we too should willingly embrace the Cross and our give up our self-centered desires.

Christians traditionally fasted on Friday as a reminder both of the sacrifice Christ made to set us free and of the need to repent and die daily to the world and our own selfish desires in order to live into the joy of God's resurrection world. In the process, we are reminded that God is still at work in our world healing wounds, feeding the hungry, setting the oppressed free, redeeming our lives.

There are many reasons to kneel at the cross daily. First, we invite God into our inner dark and hidden places that prevent us from following Christ wholeheartedly. We invite the Spirit to uncover our sins and transform us so that Christ's presence can shine through us. To do this we must uncover the wounds inflicted by rejection, inadequacy, and abuses from the past that limit our ability to relate to God and each other as God intends. We also need to repent of the self-centeredness, consumer clutter, ambition, guilt, and drive to dominate that focus us and our lives on selfish love and self-centered living and reach out for the life that Christ offers: a life of servanthood and compassion, of loving and caring for others, a life of identifying with the poor, and of considering the needs of others as more important than our own.

Secondly, images of Christ on the cross remind us that he died not just for me, but for all. The cross beckons us to reach out to all who are marginalized or separated from God, not just to identify with their suffering, but also to walk alongside them and relieve their burdens wherever possible.

Thirdly, we come to the Cross with the pain and suffering of a creation that is scarred by pollution, greed, and neglect and admit the contribution our actions have made. If we truly believe that "all things have been created through him and for him. He is before all things and in him all things hold together" (Col 1:16-17), we need to acknowledge our responsibility as God's stewards.

To come to the cross regularly is painful but not burdensome. By admitting our own pain and being willing to bear the burdens of others, we walk with Christ through the agony of crucifixion and death toward the joy of new life. The cross is our doorway into God's new resurrection-created world. What a joy and a privilege to enter the story of God in this way!

Focusing Our Thoughts

Set aside a few minutes during the day to remind yourself of Christ's incredible sacrifice for you on the cross:

- Reflect on Christ's death and resurrection and the wholeness it has brought to your life and the lives of others.
  1. Remind yourself of places in your life where you are aware of God's forgiveness and freedom.
  2. Thank God for places where you are aware that God has transformed brokenness into wholeness.
- Ask God to remind you of broken places in which you still need repentance and forgiveness. Is their restitution or reconciliation necessary:
  1. In your own life?
  2. In your relationship with others?
  3. In your stewardship of creation?
- Reflect on times through the day when you plan to give praise to God for the cross and the promise of forgiveness, reconciliation, and restoration.

Focusing Our Prayers

- Pray for a clearer knowledge of your own sin and need for repentance.

- Pray for those you may have wronged in the past.

- Pray for those whom you feel have wronged you.

- Pray for sensitivity to where others are hurting and feel wronged.

- Pray for family, friends, and those around the world who need to find God's salvation.

- Pray for countries and communities torn apart by conflict and lack of forgiveness.

- Pray for those who work for reconciliation and peace in racial conflict or war.

- Pray for those who work for restoration in situations of domestic conflict or with the marginalized.

Morning Prayer

Jesus Christ, Savior of our world,
Redeemer of all creation,
The bringer of health and wholeness,
We bless and praise your name.
You died for us and hung upon a cross,
Your blood was shed and your body broken,
So that we might be set free.
We bless and praise your name.

> *Pause to reflect on the cross and the ways you have been
> transformed because of Christ's sacrifice.*

Have mercy on us,
Son of the living God,
Healer of lepers, feeder of the hungry,
Releaser of the oppressed, bringer of wholeness,
Christ crucified, Eternal God,
Have mercy on us.

Help us to lay down our own lives daily,
And consciously take on Christ's life,
May we consider the needs of others as more important than
our own.
Teach us, Lord, to live the life of the cross.
Enable us to live a life of service and not of selfish ambition,
Empower us to reach out with compassion and care,
May we identify with the poor, the marginalized, and the vul-
nerable.
Teach us, Lord, to live the life of the cross.
Encourage us to extend ourselves in serving and loving,
Being willing to walk the extra mile,
May we reach out to all those who suffer and are in pain.
Teach us, Lord, to live the life of the cross.
Forgive us for when we discard Christ's life,
And so quickly reach for our own ways again,

For it is in dying to ourselves that we find life and enter the
   ways of your kingdom.
Teach us, Lord, to live the life of the cross.

Lamentations 3:22-33 (NLT)

The faithful love of the Lord never ends!
   His mercies never cease.
Great is his faithfulness;
   his mercies begin afresh each morning.
I say to myself, "The Lord is my inheritance;
   therefore, I will hope in him!"
The Lord is good to those who depend on him,
   to those who search for him.
So it is good to wait quietly
   for salvation from the Lord.
And it is good for people to submit at an early age
   to the yoke of his discipline:
Let them sit alone in silence
   beneath the Lord's demands.
Let them lie face down in the dust,
   for there may be hope at last.
Let them turn the other cheek to those who strike them
   and accept the insults of their enemies.
For no one is abandoned
   by the Lord forever.
Though he brings grief, he also shows compassion
   because of the greatness of his unfailing love.
For he does not enjoy hurting people
   or causing them sorrow.

God, may we submit to the yoke of your discipline.

1 Corinthians 1:18-31(Message)

The Message that points to Christ on the Cross seems like sheer silliness
to those hell bent on destruction, but for those on the way of salvation
it makes perfect sense. This is the way God works, and most powerfully
as it turns out. It's written, I'll turn conventional wisdom on its head, I'll
expose so-called experts as crackpots.

So where can you find someone truly wise, truly educated, truly intelligent in this day and age? Hasn't God exposed it all as pretentious nonsense? Since the world in all its fancy wisdom never had a clue when it came to knowing God, God in his wisdom took delight in using what the world considered dumb—preaching, of all things!—to bring those who trust him into the way of salvation.

While Jews clamor for miraculous demonstrations and Greeks go in for philosophical wisdom, we go right on proclaiming Christ, the Crucified. Jews treat this like an anti-miracle—and Greeks pass it off as absurd. But to us who are personally called by God himself—both Jews and Greeks—Christ is God's ultimate miracle and wisdom all wrapped up in one. Human wisdom is so tinny, so impotent, next to the seeming absurdity of God. Human strength can't begin to compete with God's "weakness."

Take a good look, friends, at who you were when you got called into this life. I don't see many of "the brightest and the best" among you, not many influential, not many from high-society families. Isn't it obvious that God deliberately chose men and women that the culture overlooks and exploits and abuses, chose these "nobodies" to expose the hollow pretensions of the "somebodies"? That makes it quite clear that none of you can get by with blowing your own horn before God. Everything that we have—right thinking and right living, a clean slate and a fresh start—comes from God by way of Jesus Christ. That's why we have the saying, "If you're going to blow a horn, blow a trumpet for God."

Thank you God for Jesus Christ, your ultimate miracle and wisdom all wrapped up in one.

Luke 9:20-27 (NLT)

Then he asked them, "But who do you say I am?"

Peter replied, "You are the Messiah sent from God!"

Jesus warned his disciples not to tell anyone who he was. "The Son of Man must suffer many terrible things," he said. "He will be rejected by the elders, the leading priests, and the teachers of religious law. He will be killed, but on the third day he will be raised from the dead."

Then he said to the crowd, "If any of you wants to be my follower, you must turn from your selfish ways, take up your cross daily, and follow me. If you try to hang on to your life, you will lose it. But if you give up your life for my sake, you will save it. And what do you benefit if you gain the whole world but are yourself lost or destroyed? If anyone is ashamed of me and my message, the Son of Man will be ashamed of that person when he returns in his glory and in the glory of the Father and the holy angels. I tell you the truth, some standing here right now will not die before they see the Kingdom of God."

God, we believe you sent your Son to redeem us,
Through Jesus Christ you showed us the path of life.
You led us to the Cross, where sin dies and freedom flows,
Where despair is transformed into hope,
Where pain and healing embrace.
Jesus Christ, we believe your Cross stands at the center of human history.
It is the ultimate outpouring of God's love for all humankind.
At the Cross, we are saved from our sins,
Our suffering gives birth to joy,
Our brokenness is transformed into wholeness.
We believe you ask us to lay down our lives at the foot of the cross,
To repent of our self-centered lives,
And acknowledge daily your incarnate presence within us.
We believe that we must journey with you through the agony of crucifixion,
To find true life as we give it away.
We must move through the horror of death to the joy of resurrection and new life.

Our Father in heaven, hallowed be your name. Your Kingdom come, your will be done, on earth as in heaven. Give us today our daily bread. Forgive us our sins, as we forgive those who sin against us. Lead us not into temptation, but deliver us from evil. For the kingdom, the power and the glory are yours. Now and forever. Amen.

Pause to offer specific prayers and thanksgivings.

Father God, today we lay our burdens at the foot of the cross,
Burdens we have shouldered that you did not intend.
Lord, forgive us for the pain we have given you.
We have taken lightly the sacrifice of your son,
And have turned our backs on your redemptive love.
Lord, forgive us for ways in which we have ignored your salvation.
We have become bound up in our own fears and anxieties,
We have doubted your caring concern for all our needs.
Lord, forgive us for denying your faithfulness to provide day by day.
We have fretted over seeds we have planted that have not yet begun to grow,
And forgotten that you are the one who brings growth and provides fruit.
Lord, forgive us for disregarding your generous guidance in all we do.
We strive in our independence to accomplish alone tasks you mean us to share,
And so deny the concern and support of a God who speaks through community.
Lord, forgive us for our selfish love and self-centered living.
We have abandoned the poor, the destitute, and the marginalized,
And so denied your love and compassion for all who are made in your image.
Lord, forgive us for failing to see your divine image reflected in friends and strangers.

God, we come to kneel before your cross and listen,
Open our eyes that we might be aware of your faithfulness,
Open our ears that we might hear your instruction,
Open our arms that we might share your generosity,
Open our hearts that we might be embraced by your love.

God, we have invited you into the dark and hidden places of
our lives,
We have chosen the way of the cross,
You have washed away our sins and cleansed us with your
blood.
Be with us this day in crucifixion and resurrection,
So that the light of Christ can truly shine out through every
part of us,
Amen.

Evening Prayer

God, be with us this night.
May your love poured out upon the cross surround us,
May your compassion lived out in incarnation move us,
May your life granted through resurrection sustain us,
God, be with us this night.
We come to the cross for healing, Lord,
For you alone can make us whole.
We come to the cross for forgiveness, Lord,
For you alone can set us free.
We come to the cross for reconciliation, Lord,
For you alone can make us one.

> *Pause to remind yourself of times you have been an*
> *instrument of God's forgiveness and reconciliation.*

Jesus, you came to save and heal us.
Your body was broken and blood poured out for us,
You healed the sick and raised the dead,
You went through death so that we might find life.
Jesus, you came to save and heal us.
You touched lepers and outcasts,
You stopped on the way to the rich man's daughter,
To heal a woman abandoned and despised with an issue of
    blood.
Jesus, you came to save and heal us.
You raised a poor woman's son to life,
And promised that one day all children will live a full life,
You gave your disciples power to follow in your steps.
Jesus, you came to save and heal us.
May we too be your caring hands,
Sent out to preach and to heal,
Anointing others with your loving touch.
Jesus, you came to save and heal us.

Adapted from 1 John 4: 7-12 (Message)

My beloved friends, let us continue to love each other,
Since love comes from God.
Let us love one another because God is love.
Everyone who loves experiences a relationship with God,
The person who refuses to love doesn't know the first thing
  about God.
Let us love one another because God is love.
This is how God showed his love for us:
God sent his only Son into the world so we might live through
  him.
Let us love one another because God is love.
This is the kind of love we are talking about: that God sent his
  Son to clear away our sins,
And the damage they've done to our relationship with God.
Let us love one another because God is love.
My dear, dear friends, if God loved us like this,
We certainly ought to love each other.
Let us love one another because God is love.
No one has seen God, ever. But if we love one another, God
  dwells deeply within us,
And his love becomes complete in us—perfect love!
Let us love one another because God is love.

Deuteronomy 7:7-8 (Message)

God wasn't attracted to you and didn't choose you because you were big and important—the fact is, there was almost nothing to you. He did it out of sheer love, keeping the promise he made to your ancestors. God stepped in and mightily bought you back out of that world of slavery, freed you from the iron grip of Pharaoh king of Egypt. Know this: God, your God, is God indeed, a God you can depend upon. He keeps his covenant of loyal love with those who love him and observe his commandments for a thousand generations.

God, our God, is God indeed!

Titus 3:4-7 (NLT)

But—"When God our Savior revealed his kindness and love, he saved us, not because of the righteous things we had done, but because of his mercy. He washed away our sins, giving us a new birth and new life through the Holy Spirit. He generously poured out the Spirit upon us through Jesus Christ our Savior. Because of his grace he declared us righteous and gave us confidence that we will inherit eternal life."

God has given us a new birth and new life through the Holy Spirit.

Mark 12:28-34 (CEV)

One of the teachers of the Law of Moses came up while Jesus and the Sadducees were arguing. When he heard Jesus give a good answer, he asked him, "What is the most important commandment?"

Jesus answered, "The most important one says: `People of Israel, you have only one Lord and God. You must love him with all your heart, soul, mind, and strength.' The second most important commandment says: `Love others as much as you love yourself.' No other commandment is more important than these."

The man replied, "Teacher, you are certainly right to say there is only one God. It is also true that we must love God with all our heart, mind, and strength, and that we must love others as much as we love ourselves. These commandments are more important than all the sacrifices and offerings that we could possibly make."

When Jesus saw that the man had given a sensible answer, he told him, "You are not far from God's kingdom." After this, no one dared ask Jesus any more questions.

The Nicene Creed

We believe in one God,
   the Father, the Almighty,
   maker of heaven and earth,
   of all that is, seen and unseen.
We believe in one Lord, Jesus Christ,

the only Son of God,
eternally begotten of the Father,
God from God, light from light,
true God from true God,
begotten, not made,
of one Being with the Father;
through him all things were made.
For us and for our salvation
he came down from heaven,
was incarnate of the Holy Spirit and the Virgin Mary
and became truly human.
For our sake he was crucified under Pontius Pilate;
he suffered death and was buried.
On the third day he rose again
in accordance with the Scriptures;
he ascended into heaven
and is seated at the right hand of the Father.
He will come again in glory to judge the living and the dead,
and his kingdom will have no end.
We believe in the Holy Spirit, the Lord, the giver of life,
who proceeds from the Father and the Son,
who with the Father and the Son is worshiped and glorified,
who has spoken through the prophets.
We believe in one holy catholic and apostolic Church.
We acknowledge one baptism for the forgiveness of sins.
We look for the resurrection of the dead,
and the life of the world to come. Amen.[23]

---

23. To counter a widening rift within the church, Constantine convened a council in Nicaea in 325 AD. A creed reflecting the position of Alexander and Athanasius was written and signed by a majority of the bishops. In 381 AD, a second council met in Constantinople. It adopted a revised and expanded form of the earlier creed, now called the Nicene Creed, the most ecumenical of creeds. Most Protestant churches join the Eastern Orthodox and Roman Catholic churches in affirming it.

Our Father in heaven, hallowed be your name. Your Kingdom come, your will be done, on earth as in heaven. Give us today our daily bread. Forgive us our sins, as we forgive those who sin against us. Lead us not into temptation, but deliver us from evil. For the kingdom, the power and the glory are yours. Now and forever. Amen.

Pause to offer specific prayers and thanksgivings.

God almighty, who created us from dust, today you suffered because of us,

Christ, who was scarred and disfigured on the cross, today you suffered instead of us,

Spirit, who transforms death into life, today you suffered with us,

Thank you, God, for in your suffering, we find hope.

God, our suffering God, your story gives us salvation,

Without you, the horrors of human suffering would be unbearable,

Your story of life, death, and resurrection gives all life meaning,

Thank you, God, for in your suffering, we find hope.

Because of your suffering, a new world broke into ours,

In your wounds is the hope of our wholeness,

In your scars is the promise of our redemption.

Thank you, God, for in your suffering, we find hope.

Father God, your deep and sacrificial love invites us to love our neighbors,

Christ, your redeeming love invites us to love the world with this same embracing love,

Spirit, your empowering presence invites us to love each other as we do ourselves.

Thank you, God, for in your love, we find life.

Your suffering transforms us into sons and daughters of the living God,

Your suffering frees us to love you with all our hearts and souls and strength,

Your suffering enables us to care for humankind as one family.
Thank you, God, for in your story, we find our true purpose.

God, may we reach within this night,
And uncover the sins that bind us.
May we reach without this night,
And expose the brokenness of our world.
God, may we reach upward this night,
And embrace the love of your presence.

God, grant us rest this night.
Guide our thoughts to what is true,
Guide our minds to what is good,
Guide our paths to what is right,
God, guide us this night and always.

The love of almighty God surround you,
The peace of the risen Christ indwell you,
The fellowship of the Holy Spirit unite you,
The life of the triune God be yours this night and evermore.
Amen.

Saturday

Discipleship and the Call to Live in God's Kingdom

The Vatican City, with the majestic dome of St Peter's Basilica at its heart, dominates the modern city of Rome. To the north is that favorite of all visitors to Rome, the gigantic Vatican museum, with its four exhausting miles of displays. In the basement is an almost deserted room filled with sarcophagi from the first through third centuries. Here chiseled in stone on the coffins of long-forgotten people of faith are the most exciting images of rejoicing and fulfillment I have ever seen. Christ, sitting on a donkey, making his triumphal way into Jerusalem, confronted me at every turn. Swirling around him are rejoicing throngs of people waving palm branches. The disabled are raising their crutches above their heads as they are healed, hungry people are being fed with fish and bread, and in the corner a man is rising from the dead.

What will God's resurrection-created world look like? Obviously, that is a question none of us can really answer, but as I looked at these exciting images of Jesus, I had a fairly good idea. Jesus doesn't just reveal God to us, he also shows us what God's new world is like. Through his words and actions, we catch glimpses of a transformed world in which all barriers of race and class are removed. It transforms hate into love, scarcity into abundance, greed into generosity, violence into peace, and oppression into justice and equality. In God's new world, all lines of separation are erased, the hungry are fed, the oppressed set free, and we are invited into a new creation of wholeness and healing, of redemption and renewal.

Just as Jesus' life was inspired by the in-breaking of God's resurrection world, so were the lives of the early disciples. They left homes and jobs and family. They turned their backs on the values of Roman and Greek culture and embraced God's new world and its values of love and mutual care because they believed that in the coming of Christ this new world had broken into ours. They believed that their primary allegiance was no longer to the kings and rulers of this world, but to Christ. Through baptism they had become citizens of God's new world. Their vision became this dream of shalom, wholeness, and restoration fulfilled in Christ—a vision of all people, including the dispossessed, the excluded, and the needy, drawn under Christ's lordship into a single family. Their vision became one in which all persons find a place of abundant provision in a new community that is loving, caring, and mutually supportive. They saw all humanity as heirs of a single hope and bearers of a single destiny—the restoration, care, and management of all God's creation in a new heaven and a new earth. Their purpose had become the in-breaking of this new world into the lives of those with whom they met and interacted.

This is the same vision and purpose that has inspired followers of Christ throughout the ages. It motivated the Celtic saint Brigit to feed thousands each day from the monastery at Kildare and led Francis of Assisi to give up his wealth and privilege to work among the poor. It inspired John Wesley in the eighteenth century to not only preach to the poor, but to become a leader in many social justice issues. It led William Wilberforce to fight against slavery and Elizabeth Fry to visit prisons in nineteenth-century England.

Central to God's resurrection world is what James calls "the royal law": love of God and love of neighbor. The culture of God's new world is one of mutual care and concern, and the language is the language of love. NT Wright expresses it this way:

> Love is not a duty; it is our destiny. It is the language that Jesus spoke and we are called to speak it so that we can converse with him. It is the food that they eat in God's new world, and we must acquire a taste for it here and now. It is the music God has written for all his creatures to sing and we are called to learn it and practice it now."[24]

Incredibly, Jesus also invites us to join these early disciples and the great clouds of witnesses throughout the ages who have lived as representatives of this new world. Together with all followers of Christ, God asks us to join in the exciting drama of seeing the world changed now in partial ways in anticipation of the day when Christ returns and all things are indeed made whole.

---

24. Wright, *Surprised By Hope*, 288.

Focusing our Thoughts

Set aside a few minutes during the day to meditate on your vision of God's new resurrection-created world and of those saints past and present who lived as citizens of this new world:

- Center your thoughts on the promise of Christ's return and the eternal world in which all creation is restored, reconciled, and made whole.

- Reflect on ways God could use you to model the in-breaking of this new world of wholeness and abundance.

- Thank God for those who have guided your Christian walk:

  1. For friends and family who have influenced your life.

  2. For mentors and teachers who have provided godly models for your life.

  3. For Christian saints, past or present, who were examples to you because they followed Christ and committed themselves to God's kingdom purposes.

- Mentally picture times throughout the day when you plan to pause and pray for the in-breaking of God's resurrection-created world.

Focusing our Prayers

- Pray for places where you see God's eternal world breaking into ours:

  1. Through the work of the church and non-profit organizations.

  2. Through those that work in your community.

  3. Through local and global mission.

- Pray for those who need to see God's eternal world break into their present situations:

  1. In healing for the sick, particularly those with malaria, AIDS, and TB.

  2. In justice particularly for those whose exploitation we benefit from even though we may not create it.

  3. In abundance for those who are hungry and live in poverty

  4. In peace for the victims of war and conflict.

  5. In freedom for those imprisoned physically, emotionally or spiritually.

- Pray for those who are persecuted because of their faith.

- Pray for organizations and ministries you know that reflect glimpses of God's new world:

  1. For international and local mission organizations.

  2. For those involved in peacekeeping and ministries of reconciliation.

  3. For those who work with refugees and displaced persons.

  4. For those who work with the hungry locally and globally.

Morning Prayer

A new day dawning, and God is with us,
In its light, may we see God's light,
In its sounds, may we hear God's voice,
In its unfolding, may we find God's purpose.
Blessed Lord Jesus, may we live today in the hope of your new world.
The promise of wholeness and completeness is ours,
The peace of abundance for all you leave with us,
Alleluia! We awake to the glory of your resurrection-created world.

Grace and peace to all God's people,
From the one who is, who always was, and who will always be.
Peace from God's Spirit and from Jesus Christ the faithful witness to these things,
The first to rise from the dead, and the ruler of all the nations of the world.
All glory to him who loves us and freed us from our sins,
All glory to the one who shed his blood for us.
He has made us a company of priests for God our Creator.
All glory and power to him forever and ever!

> *Pause to remind yourself of people that have provided godly examples for you.*

God, you set us free, free to love you with all our hearts and souls and minds,
You set us free to love our neighbors as we do ourselves.
God, you call us to the freedom of your eternal world today.
Free us from our self-centeredness and indifference and greed,
Free us to share generously of your bounty so others will not hunger or lack provision.
God, you call us to the freedom of your eternal world today.
Free us to live in love and compassion and mutual care,

May we accept your gift and enter the wholeness of your
resurrection-created world today.
God, you call us to the freedom of your eternal world today.

Psalm 145:8-13 (NLT)

The Lord is merciful and compassionate,
  slow to get angry and filled with unfailing love.
The Lord is good to everyone.
He showers compassion on all his creation.
All of your works will thank you, Lord,
  and your faithful followers will praise you.
They will speak of the glory of your kingdom;
  they will give examples of your power.
They will tell about your mighty deeds
  and about the majesty and glory of your reign.
For your kingdom is an everlasting kingdom.
  You rule throughout all generations.
The Lord always keeps his promises;
  he is gracious in all he does

God always keeps his promises and is gracious in all he does.

Isaiah 65:17-25 (Message)

Pay close attention now: I'm creating new heavens and a new earth.
All the earlier troubles, chaos, and pain are things of the past, to be
forgotten.
Look ahead with joy. Anticipate what I'm creating:
I'll create Jerusalem as sheer joy, create my people as pure delight.
I'll take joy in Jerusalem, take delight in my people:
No more sounds of weeping in the city, no cries of anguish; no more
babies dying in the cradle, or old people who don't enjoy a full lifetime;
One-hundredth birthdays will be considered normal—
They'll build houses and move in.
They'll plant fields and eat what they grow.

No more building a house that some outsider takes over, no more plant-
ing fields that some enemy confiscates, for my people will be as long-
lived as trees, my chosen ones will have satisfaction in their work.

They won't work and have nothing come of it, they won't have children snatched out from under them.

For they themselves are plantings blessed by God, with their children and grandchildren likewise God-blessed. Before they call out, I'll answer. Before they've finished speaking, I'll have heard. Wolf and lamb will graze the same meadow, lion and ox eat straw from the same trough, but snakes—they'll get a diet of dirt! Neither animal nor human will hurt or kill anywhere on my Holy Mountain," says God.

Praise God who is making all things new!

Matthew 5:3-16 (NLT)

God blesses those who are poor and realize their need for him, for the Kingdom of Heaven is theirs. God blesses those who mourn, for they will be comforted. God blesses those who are humble, for they will inherit the whole earth. God blesses those who hunger and thirst for justice,   for they will be satisfied. God blesses those who are merciful,   for they will be shown mercy. God blesses those whose hearts are pure,   for they will see God. God blesses those who work for peace,   for they will be called the children of God. God blesses those who are persecuted for doing right,   for the Kingdom of Heaven is theirs.

"God blesses you when people mock you and persecute you and lie about you and say all sorts of evil things against you because you are my followers. Be happy about it! Be very glad! For a great reward awaits you in heaven. And remember, the ancient prophets were persecuted in the same way.

"You are the salt of the earth. But what good is salt if it has lost its flavor? Can you make it salty again? It will be thrown out and trampled under-foot as worthless.

"You are the light of the world—like a city on a hilltop that cannot be hidden. No one lights a lamp and then puts it under a basket. Instead, a lamp is placed on a stand, where it gives light to everyone in the house. In the same way, let your good deeds shine out for all to see, so that everyone will praise your heavenly Father."

May our good deeds shine out for all to see.

God, we believe we are Christ's representatives,
Citizens of a resurrection-created world.
We believe and trust in God's kingdom coming,
A new world breaking onto ours.
God, we believe we are called to be the salt of the earth,
We are your light shining into the darkness.
We believe and trust in God's kingdom coming,
A new world breaking onto ours.
We believe the poor will be fed and the prisoners set free,
The blind will see and the deaf hear.
We believe and trust in God's kingdom coming,
A new world breaking onto ours.
We believe there will be no more tears or crying or pain,
The sick will be healed and the lame leap for joy.
We believe and trust in God's kingdom coming,
A new world breaking onto ours.
We believe in God's eternal world of wholeness, love, and joy,
Where justice and righteousness will have no end.
We believe and trust in God's kingdom coming,
A new world breaking onto ours.
We believe we will live in fellowship with God and each other,
With abundance, peace, and fulfillment for all creation.
We believe and trust in God's kingdom coming,
A new world breaking onto ours.

Our Father in heaven, hallowed be your name. Your King-
dom come, your will be done, on earth as in heaven. Give us
today our daily bread. Forgive us our sins, as we forgive those
who sin against us. Lead us not into temptation, but deliver
us from evil. For the kingdom, the power and the glory are
yours. Now and forever. Amen

Pause to offer specific prayers and thanksgivings.

May we enter God's kingdom of wholeness and completeness,
May we be instruments of God's peace today.

Where there is despair, may we bring God's vision of hope,
May we be instruments of God's wholeness today.
Where there is war, may we bring glimpses of peace,
May we be instruments of God's shalom today.
Where there is sickness, may we do acts of healing,
May we be instruments of God's peace today.
Where there is oppression, may we bring the promise of free-
dom,
May we be instruments of God's wholeness today.
Where there is hunger, may we share from our bounty,
May we be instruments of God's shalom today.
Through our words and actions, may we represent God's
resurrection-created world.
Lord, may we love our neighbors as we do ourselves.

Go into the world knowing you are touched by the Triune God,
Let your life shine with the holiness of God,
Let your heart be transformed by the peace of Christ,
Let your ways be filled with the joy of the spirit.

May we live in a manner worthy of the gospel of Christ,
May we live as citizens of God's resurrection-created world.
May our love increase so that it overflows to friend and
stranger,
May God strengthen our hearts so that we will be blameless
in thought and deed,
May Christ's holiness enter our lives so that we can join the
company of his holy saints,
May we please God so that together with all followers of
Jesus we can rejoice in eternal life.
Amen.

Evening Prayer

God of peace,
God of rest,
God of quiet,
Refresh us this night,
Enclose us with your love,
Calm us with your spirit.

Lord, we call on you, for you will answer us,
And give ear to our prayers.
We will lie down and sleep in peace, for you alone make us
dwell in safety.
Keep us in your unending love,
And hide us under the shadow of your wings.
We will lie down and sleep in peace, for you alone make us
dwell in safety.
Show us the wonder of your mercy,
And surround us with your arms of compassion.
We will lie down and sleep in peace, for you alone make us
dwell in safety.

> *Pause to reflect on the places in which you have demon-*
> *strated God's kingdom values today.*

God, the week is ended,
And we place it in your hands,
We place it in your hands.
Its fears and its anxieties,
The broken places it has exposed,
We place them in your hands.
Things that clutter and consume,
Attitudes that separate and divide,
We place them in your hands.
Its hurts and its failures,
The pain it has uncovered,

We place them in your hands.
The healing we have found,
The compassion we have shown,
We place them in your hands.
Its joys and celebration,
The love it has embraced,
We place them in your hands.

Adapted from Psalm 139 (Message)

You have looked deep into our hearts O Lord,
You know all about us,
You know when we are resting and when we are working,
From heaven you discover our thoughts.
You notice everything we do and everywhere we go,
Before we even speak, you know what we will say,
Nothing about us is hidden from you,
Even before we were born, you had written in your book
    what we would do.
Everything you do is marvelous—of this we have no doubt,
We praise you for the wonderful way you created us,
Your thoughts are precious to us, O God!
Your purposes are far beyond our imagining.

Hebrews 12:1-13 (Message)

Do you see what this means—all these pioneers who blazed the way, all these veterans cheering us on? It means we'd better get on with it. Strip down, start running—and never quit! No extra spiritual fat, no parasitic sins. Keep your eyes on Jesus, who both began and finished this race we're in. Study how he did it. Because he never lost sight of where he was headed—that exhilarating finish in and with God—he could put up with anything along the way: Cross, shame, whatever. And now he's there, in the place of honor, right alongside God. When you find yourselves flagging in your faith, go over that story again, item by item, that long litany of hostility he plowed through. That will shoot adrenaline into your souls!

In this all-out match against sin, others have suffered far worse than you, to say nothing of what Jesus went through—all that bloodshed! So don't feel sorry for yourselves. Or have you forgotten how good parents treat children, and that God regards you as his children?

My dear child, don't shrug off God's discipline, but don't be crushed by it either. It's the child he loves that he disciplines; the child he embraces, he also corrects. God is educating you; that's why you must never drop out. He's treating you as dear children. This trouble you're in isn't punishment; it's training, the normal experience of children. Only irresponsible parents leave children to fend for themselves. Would you prefer an irresponsible God? We respect our own parents for training and not spoiling us, so why not embrace God's training so we can truly live? While we were children, our parents did what seemed best to them. But God is doing what is best for us, training us to live God's holy best. At the time, discipline isn't much fun. It always feels like it's going against the grain. Later, of course, it pays off handsomely, for it's the well-trained who find themselves mature in their relationship with God.

So don't sit around on your hands! No more dragging your feet! Clear the path for long-distance runners so no one will trip and fall, so no one will step in a hole and sprain an ankle. Help each other out. And run for it!

May we keep our eyes on Jesus who began and finished the race we are in.

Revelation 21:1-5 (Message)

I saw Heaven and earth new-created. Gone the first Heaven, gone the first earth, gone the sea. I saw Holy Jerusalem, new-created, descending resplendent out of Heaven, as ready for God as a bride for her husband. I heard a voice thunder from the Throne: "Look! Look! God has moved into the neighborhood, making his home with men and women! They're his people, he's their God. He'll wipe every tear from their eyes. Death is gone for good—tears gone, crying gone, pain gone—all the first order of things gone." The Enthroned continued, "Look! I'm making everything new. Write it all down—each word dependable and accurate."

Look! Look! God had moved into the neighborhood and made his home with us!

Mark 4:26-32 (NLT)

Jesus also said, "The Kingdom of God is like a farmer who scatters seed on the ground. Night and day, while he's asleep or awake, the seed sprouts and grows, but he does not understand how it happens. The earth produces the crops on its own. First a leaf blade pushes through, then the heads of wheat are formed, and finally the grain ripens. And as soon as the grain is ready, the farmer comes and harvests it with a sickle, for the harvest time has come."

Jesus said, "How can I describe the Kingdom of God? What story should I use to illustrate it? It is like a mustard seed planted in the ground. It is the smallest of all seeds, but it becomes the largest of all garden plants; it grows long branches, and birds can make nests in its shade."

With saints of all ages, we come to God this night,
With those who were, who are, and who will come,
With saints of all ages,
We believe and trust in God the creator,
The one who is, who always was, and who is still to come,
The one who calls us to be salt in a world that has lost flavor.
With saints of all ages,
We believe and trust in Christ our Savior,
The first to rise from the dead, and the ruler of all the nations
 of the world,
The one who calls us to be light in a world that is mired by
 darkness.
With saints of all ages,
We believe and trust in the life-giving Spirit,
The seal of our inheritance the guarantee of what is to come,
Who calls us to glorify God through our words and actions.
With saints of all ages,
We believe and trust in God's kingdom coming,
A new world breaking onto ours, eternal world of wholeness
 and joy,
Where the poor will be fed and the prisoners set free.
With saints of all ages,
We believe and trust in God's kingdom coming,

Where justice and righteousness will have no end,
Where the sick will be healed, the blind see and the deaf hear.
With saints of all ages,
We believe and trust in God.

Our Father in heaven, hallowed be your name. Your Kingdom come, your will be done, on earth as in heaven. Give us today our daily bread. Forgive us our sins, as we forgive those who sin against us. Lead us not into temptation, but deliver us from evil. For the kingdom, the power and the glory are yours. Now and forever. Amen.

Pause to offer specific prayers and thanksgivings.

As this day ends, we close out the week,
Knowing we have been touched by the Triune God,
May our lives shine with the love of God,
May our hearts be transformed by the compassion of Christ,
May our ways be filled with the peace of the Spirit.

God, the week is ending and you are with us.
Come down, God of life, fill us with your love.
Come in, Christ of peace, anoint us with your compassion.
Come among us, Spirit of joy, teach us to celebrate your ways.

God, the week is ending and you are with us.
You draw us into your presence, so that we can hear your
   voice.
You ask us to listen, so that we can know your ways.
You send us out to serve, so that we can be your people.

Let us go forth,
In the goodness of our merciful Father,
In the gentleness of our brother Jesus,
In the radiance of the Holy Spirit,
In the faith of the apostles,
In the Joyful praise of the angels,
In the holiness of the saints,

In the courage of the martyrs.
Let us go forth,
In the wisdom of our all-seeing Father,
In the patience of our all-loving brother,
In the truth of the all-knowing Spirit,
In the learning of the apostles,
In the gracious guidance of the angels,
In the patience of the saints,
In the self-control of the martyrs,
Such is the path for all servants of Christ,
The path from death to eternal life.[25]

Lord God, you have called your servants to ventures of which we cannot see the ending, by paths as yet untrod, through perils unknown. Give us faith to go knowing not where we go, but that your hand is leading us and your love sustaining us; through Jesus Christ our Lord.[26]
Amen.

---

25. "The Rising," an Ancient Celtic prayer

26. Prayer written by Eric Milner-White, "Service of Evening Prayer," *Lutheran Book of Worship*, 153.

Christine Sine is the Executive Director of Mustard Seed Associates (www.msainfo.org). She trained as a physician in Australia and developed the medical ministry for Mercy Ships. She now lives in Seattle with her husband Tom Sine as part of the Mustard Seed House community (mustardseedhouse. wordpress.com). She is an avid gardener with a growing passion to enable followers of Christ to connect their faith to everyday life. She speaks on issues relating to how to change our timestyle and lifestyle to develop a more spiritual rhythm for life that interweaves throughout every aspect of life. She has authored several books including *Godspace* and *Living on Purpose*. She blogs at godspace.wordpress.com.

Mustard Seed Associates is a small non-profit organization that raises awareness of challenges Christians will face in life, church and community in the future. We seek to foster spirituality that draws followers of Christ into a deeper relationship with God and encourage innovation that enables us to create new ways to advance God's kingdom purposes and engage tomorrow's challenges. MSA is also a crossroads, grassroots organization—connecting people across generations, denominations and cultures and equipping them to creatively transform their cultures by both living differently and making a difference for God's kingdom. For more information visit our website at www.msainfo.org.

Other MSA Resources

E-books and Media

To Garden With God
by Christine Sine

A manual for backyard organic gardening prepared by Christine Sine for spring workshops. This resource mixes practical advice with spiritual reflections on creation and God's great bounty.

Turbulent Times—Ready or Not!
by Tom Sine

In these changing economic times, how can churches and individuals better respond to the needs of vulnerable neighbors and be good stewards of their resources?

Justice at the Table
by Ricci Kilmer

This resource is a collection of personal reflections and practical ideas to help us redeem "food" in all its dimensions—from its mundane place as an annoying chore to a spiritual practice essential to a life of faith. Take a look and see how you can continue to redeem your relationship with food for the kingdom of God.

A Journey Into Wholeness: Lenten Reflection Guide
by Christine Sine

A five-week study with reflections, litanies, and activities exploring our brokenness and the suffering of Jesus Christ as he journeyed toward the cross.

A Journey Into God's Resurrection-Created World: An Easter Celebration Guide
by Christine Sine

In these changing economic times, how can churches and individuals better respond to the needs of vulnerable neighbors and be good stewards of their resources?

Advent Reflection Videos
by Christine Sine

Every year, Christine creates another meditation on the coming of Christ. Titles include "The Coming of the Lord Is Near," "Waiting for the Light," and "Awaiting the Christ Child." Available at stores.lulu.com/mail1058

Recordings from Past Events

Did you miss our conferences the past few years? For just a couple bucks you can hear from Shane Claiborne, Efrem Smith, Lisa Domke, Mark Scandrette, Eliacin Rosario-Cruz, just to name a few. Available at stores.lulu.com/mail1058

Books by MSA Staff

Available at www.msainfo.org/store

Godspace: Time for Peace in the Rhythms of Life
by Christine Sine (Barclay Books, 2006)

Living On Purpose: Finding God's Best for Your Life
by Christine and Tom Sine (Baker Books, 2002)

Travel Well: Maintaining Physical, Spiritual, and Emotional Health During International Ministry
by Christine Aroney-Sine, M.D. (World Vision, 2005)

Tales of a Seasick Doctor: Life Aboard a Mercy Ship
by Christine Aroney-Sine, M.D. (Zondervan, 1996)

The New Conspirators: Creating the Future One Mustard Seed at a Time
by Tom Sine (InterVarsity Press, 2008)

Mustard Seed vs McWorld: Reinventing Life and Faith for the Future
by Tom Sine (Baker Books, 1999)

CPSIA information can be obtained at www.ICGtesting.com
Printed in the USA
LVOW131308290712

292018LV00001B/39/P